THE PRINCIPLE OF 18

ALSO BY EYAL N. DANON:

THE GOLDEN KEY OF GANGOTRI

BEFORE THE KIDS AND MORTGAGE:
ONE COUPLE'S ESCAPE FROM THE ORDINARY

THE PRINCIPLE OF 18

Getting the Most Out of Every Stage of Your Life

EYAL N. DANON

The Principle of 18:
Getting the Most Out of Every Stage of Your Life
© 2022, Eyal N. Danon

All rights reserved.
Published by Blue Branch Press, Tenafly, NJ

ISBN 978-1-7362994-4-9 (paperback)
ISBN 978-1-7362994-5-6 (eBook)
Library of Congress Control Number: 2021922846

Without limiting the rights under copyright reserved above, no part of this publication may be reproduced, stored in or introduced into a retrieval system, or transmitted in any form or by any means (electronic, mechanical, photocopying, recording or otherwise whether now or hereafter known), without the prior written permission of both the copyright owner and the above publisher of this book, except by a reviewer who wishes to quote brief passages in connection with a review written for insertion in a magazine, newspaper, broadcast, website, blog or other outlet in conformity with United States and International Fair Use or comparable guidelines to such copyright exceptions.

This book is intended to provide accurate information with regard to its subject matter and reflects the opinion and perspective of the author. However, in times of rapid change, ensuring all information provided is entirely accurate and up-to-date at all times is not always possible. Therefore, the author and publisher accept no responsibility for inaccuracies or omissions and specifically disclaim any liability, loss or risk, personal, professional or otherwise, which may be incurred as a consequence, directly or indirectly, of the use and/or application of any of the contents of this book.

Publishing consultant: David Wogahn for AuthorImprints.com

To my parents, Joseph and Joheved Danon

*Our deepest fears are like dragons
guarding our deepest treasures.*
— Rainer Maria Rilka

TABLE OF CONTENTS

Acknowledgments i
Introduction: Timing Your Life for Success 1
The Dreamer: Imagining Your Future 11
  Childhood to 18
    North Star 13
    Backyard Blues 16
    Escape from Devil's Island 18
    Dream Killers 20
    How to Dream 22
    How many dreams should you have? 28
    The Right Mentor 35
    The Interviews 38
    Transition Plan: From Dreamer to Explorer 39
    Key Ideas for Dreamers 42

The Explorer: The Adventure Begins 43
  18 to 36
    North Star 45
    Inside Megiddo Prison 48
    Minimize Your Regrets 58
    Macho's Cholesterol-Free Eggs 62

Let's Talk About Money 64
The Journey Ahead 66
A Gentle Push 68
The Weed Garden 70
Discovery of the Lost City 73
Follow Your Own Path 75
Messy Endings 77
Transition Plan: From Explorer to Builder 81
Key Ideas for Explorers 84

The Builder: The Joy of Achievement 85
From 36 to 54

North Star 87
Ride the Success Train 90
Play to your Strengths 92
Taking Risks 94
Ray and the Worm 99
Better than your Immediate Competition 101
Playing Chicken 103
The Longest Commute 108
The Walk of Shame 111
A Winning Approach 113
Transition Plan 115
Key Ideas for Builders 118

The Mentor: Sharing Your Knowledge 119
54 to 72

North Star 121
On Becoming a Mentor 123
Dan from Turnberry 125
Don't Retire Early without a Plan 127

My Mentors 129

Making the Switch 132

New Identities 135

Transition Plan 137

Key Ideas for Mentors 139

The Giver: Taking the High Road 141
72 to 90 and Beyond

North Star 143

Beyond the Golf Community 145

Finding Purpose 146

Safe Water, Free Books, and Personal Loans 148

A Starting Point 150

Key Ideas for Givers 154

Epilogue: Connecting the Generations 155
About the Author 159

ACKNOWLEDGMENTS

This book wouldn't have been possible without the help and encouragement of my family. They kept pushing me to complete the manuscript and gave me the time and space to do so.

My fabulous editing team, Christine Moore, Meghan Pinson and Ruth Thaler-Carter, provided sage advice and recommendations that dramatically elevated the book to another level while keeping a keen eye on flow and coherence. My talented consultant, David Wogahn, a wise wizard in the mysterious world of publishing. Dr. Tamara Altman helped with psychological research, expertly weaving in the most relevant research findings in support of my theories. Shani Boianjiu, author of the novel *The People of Forever Are Not Afraid*, provided timely and relevant comments.

To all my own Mentors and Givers who have made my journey possible without expecting anything else in return: You have my heartfelt appreciation and gratitude. You kept pushing me in the right direction while offering support and encouragement in times of struggle, and I hope this book conveys the immense debt that I owe to all of you.

To my coaching clients throughout the years, your amazing experiences and willingness to share them with me on a weekly basis provided much of the content for this project. Your ability to change course and continue to redefine yourselves at different points of your life is a source of inspiration to me.

INTRODUCTION
Timing Your Life for Success

The Principle of 18 is an original and unconventional life-design system for getting the most out of every stage of your life. In a frantic world, where so many people feel stressed and unfulfilled, this unique system provides peace of mind through a structured approach to life's major transitions, enabling you to achieve your goals while sustaining a deep sense of purpose. You can do this by realizing the potential of five stages: the Dreamer, Explorer, Builder, Mentor, and Giver. Each stage lasts for 18 years, and every stage is interconnected.

Following this system will minimize your regrets, decrease your worries, and enable you to lead a joyous, meaningful life. You will be able to fulfill your personal goals and make a difference in the lives of others and your larger community in due time. This modular approach ensures that you will not waste precious opportunities when they count the most, and that you'll avoid making serious mistakes along the way.

The first of the five life stages in the 18 Principle is the Dreamer, from birth to age 18, when you focus on identifying empowering dreams and learning how to flesh them out. In the second stage, as the Explorer from age 18 to 36, you learn how to commit to serious exploration in search of the one area you are passionate about and can excel at.

In the Builder stage, from 36 to 54, you focus on creating your own empire while not forgetting to have fun along the way. In the Mentor stage, from 54 to 72, you continue to work while guiding the younger generations. At 72, as a Giver, you remain relevant by dedicating yourself to a community-based initiative.

FIGURE 1: THE FIVE LIFE STAGES

Birth to 18	18 to 36	36 to 54	54 to 72	72 to 90
Dreamer ⇒	Explorer ⇒	Builder ⇒	Mentor ⇒	Giver

Following the Principle of 18 enables people in their twenties to fully explore their life choices, work for only 18 years in their thirties and forties, and share the wisdom and experiences they've gained when they reach their mid-fifties. The key to this entire system is completing each stage of life with utter joy, without draining yourself in the process.

Life is meant to be enjoyed *right now*, wherever you are on your journey. Find joy in charting compelling visions for your future self in the Dreamer phase, enjoy carefree years while you search for your unique path in the Explorer phase, and feel the satisfaction of creating something valuable in the Builder years, which lead to the Mentor phase and the joy of teaching others how to achieve their goals while avoiding costly mistakes along the way. The ultimate joy comes in the final chapter of life, when you find the cause that is nearest and dearest to your heart and can focus on giving back with pure intent.

Introduction

As a Columbia University Certified Life Coach and the founder of Ignite Advisory Group, a consulting company that serves thirty percent of the Fortune 500 firms, I have mentored people from all backgrounds on how to get the most out of their lives. It all comes down to the ability to change course, nail the transitions, and see options where others see unbreachable walls. The Principle of 18 presents a new model for human development, one that goes against the grain in a frenzied culture hooked on instant gratification and short-term perspectives.

Our goal is to clarify what to focus on during any given period in our lives. This system anchors us by telling us what is profoundly important at any of the five life stages, how best to prepare for the next transition, and how to leverage the help of those who have walked the path before us. We know what we need to do, and we do not have to worry about pursuing goals that belong to other life stages.

Following this system will allow you to experience life fully, from different vantage points and with a specific mindset, without being stuck in the same stage all your life. Each phase builds on the momentum of the previous one. By making deliberate changes, you can ensure that your life is never boring—because you'll be able to reinvent yourself five times during your lifetime.

I am sure you've heard the phrase "timing is everything" hundreds of times. Most people use it in a narrow context, like when they grab the last fresh bagel from the deli or the bus shows up exactly as they reach the stop. But these are trivial examples. Taking a profoundly long-term perspective on your entire life—from childhood to old age—has the potential to transform the arc of your life's journey.

Sounds easy enough, but most of us get it wrong. For example, we try to make money at the beginning of our careers, when we are least prepared and knowledgeable. In doing so we lose the opportunities afforded to us in our precious youth to find the one area we should dedicate our working years to. Years later, when we get to our mid-fifties and are still in our working years, we often miss a priceless opportunity to mentor younger people and share what we have learned along the way. Lost in our everyday struggles, we can barely find time to rise above the daily grind and see past the chaos that our lives have come to represent. What we lack is a persistent plan of attack for what to do and when, throughout our entire life span.

How exactly does the Principle of 18 work? Many of us go through life wishing we had a manual that would tell us what to do *now*, and more importantly, how to prepare for what comes next. Without a blueprint, we're trying our best to make sense of what is going on around us. What I have seen in my own life and in my coaching practice is that quite often, we are not thinking about the bigger picture. We get lost in our daily routines and habits and start sleepwalking through life, with no guiding belief about where we should focus our energies and what we should aim for. This autopilot mode robs us of the power to achieve extraordinary things.

Each stage identified in the Principle of 18 provides specific learning opportunities. The Dreamer (our first 18 years) focuses on identifying your dreams, charting a detailed process for realizing them, and creating a compelling vision for your future—for the person you could become. In the Explorer stage, you'll fully explore your dreams and aspirations, even if it takes many years to do so.

Most of us are out of the gate too early, trying to make hay while we can, taking on jobs we shouldn't accept and burying our chances of escape from the average life. What do we *usually* do in the Explorer phase? We try to learn a profession or trade, make a living, start a family, pay the bills, and worry about making it in the real world. Sometimes, yes, we get lucky, and things work out as we hope they will. But just as often, we spend a lot of time and expend a good deal of energy traveling the wrong path. We constantly compare ourselves to the people around us, and we are always rushing it. We get out of school and plunge into the first job that comes along or grab at the first opportunity that presents itself before we've determined whether it's what we *really* want to do with our lives—and certainly before we've acquired the skills and mindset to do it exceptionally well.

The Explorer stage is about discovering the one area you can excel at—while getting an education and possibly raising a family. Get ready for busy, exciting times!

The next life stage is the Builder. During the 18 years from age 36 to 54, you can focus on building your own empire. These are the years when you can fully leverage your unique talents. If you plan it right, you will not need to work as hard after this stage. Although it does take a focused effort to create a solid foundation for the rest of your life, it shouldn't take more than 18 years if you have a solid plan and are smart about the way you implement it.

A good symbol for the Builder stage is the moso, a bamboo plant that grows in China. After the moso is planted, no visible growth occurs for up to five years, even under ideal conditions. Then, as if by magic, it suddenly begins growing at the rate of nearly two and a half feet per day, reaching its full height of ninety feet within six weeks. But it's not magic. The moso's rapid growth is due to the miles of roots it developed during those first five long years!

Despite what most people experience, we are not designed to work hard all our lives. What is the point, anyway? Aren't 18 years of hard work enough? How long do you need to do something at such a high level of commitment? Hard work carries the day, but the day must have clear boundaries. It's not something that goes on forever. The Builder stage is characterized by a strong focus on getting things done and making progress while being true to yourself and keeping your sense of humor.

The Mentor stage in your mid-fifties provides an exceptional opportunity to raise your head and shift gears again—by guiding Dreamers, Explorers, and Builders.

Finally, from age 72 to 90, the Giver stage puts your focus on giving back. It is simple as that. This is your chance to leave a legacy, to help create a better future for the next generation. Use your knowledge, passion, and finances to advance the cause that is closest to your heart. This last stage of life is all about generosity and compassion.

Interestingly, the number 18 has special significance in many cultures and religions.

- In the Jewish tradition, it is the number signifying life. According to the Kabbalah, the number 18 bestows extraordinary good luck, and it is recommended to use the power of this number whenever possible in your

life. Jews even give monetary gifts in multiples of 18, blessing the recipient with a long, lucky life.
- In Christianity, it is the number of years missing from the life of Jesus Christ.
- In Hinduism, it is considered the code number for breaking into the mystery of the universe; the *Bhagavad Gita*, Hinduism's holiest scripture, is 18 chapters long, as is the first Veda.
- In China and Japan, 18 is a significant token of good luck.
- In Islam, the thirteenth-century Sufi mystic Rumi composed 18 verses for the introduction of his iconic teaching verse, the *Masnavi*.

Although this system works best if you start at the beginning of your life and move through the phases, we rarely operate under ideal conditions, and you're probably reading this book after having turned 18—perhaps long after. You can still use the power of the Principle at any stage of your life, even if you are already in the Mentor or Giver phases, by applying the lessons from this book to your own life in an accelerated way. After all, at the Mentor and Giver phases, you have the benefit of a lifetime of dreaming, exploring, and building to reflect on. You can take advantage of the fact that you have "been there, done that" to create a compelling new vision for your future and follow the steps outlined in this book to reach your objectives. Instead of having full periods of 18 years for each life stage, you can concentrate your stages using your unique experience and judgment to fast-track to your goals.

If you are reading this book in your twenties, thirties, or forties, this model will allow you to maximize your potential and drastically decrease your worries. You'll be able to build on the energy of your previous life stages and time your next one without losing a beat. After all, the universe is constantly changing, growing, dying, and being renewed and reborn. The Bible tells us that "for everything, there is a season, and a time for every purpose under heaven," but also that "whatsoever a man soweth, that shall he also reap." Too many of us attempt to reap before we have sown our seeds.

Living according to the Principle of 18 will guarantee that you don't waste a lot of time negotiating a road strewn with potholes or building castles on shifting sands. Instead, you'll use the first 36 years of your life to dream, explore, earn an education, build a family, and learn about yourself and your chosen profession. By the time you *do* launch into your career, you'll have a sturdy foundation upon which to build a satisfying and successful future that allows you to move into the Mentor and Giver phases in due time.

This approach gives you the freedom to act on what you need to over the long term and in the right order. It grants you the freedom to be yourself and the confidence that you have time to master the lessons of each stage before moving on to the next. The five stages of life I outline in this book may seem black-and-white, but they represent a map that can guide you on your own journey. The truth is that at *every* stage, we dream, explore, build, mentor, and give. As figure 2 demonstrates, the difference is simply in how much weight you give to the dominant theme of each one.

Life is constantly challenging and testing us. Not to see whether you're better than your friends or co-workers, but to test your own limits, to see if you can become the best version of yourself at each stage of your life. For example, if you are in your mid-twenties, myriad things vie for your attention every day. You need a North Star to remind yourself "I am an Explorer now above all else, and that's what I need to focus on during these important years."

Each chapter in this book opens with a North Star—what this stage of life is all about and what you need to pay attention to as you embark on it. Each chapter ends with a Transition Plan that identifies key concepts for you to focus on as you switch gears into the next life stage. These transition periods begin three years before each new life stage, and they provide a safe zone for reflection, planning, and changing your mindset in preparation for the next major life transition.

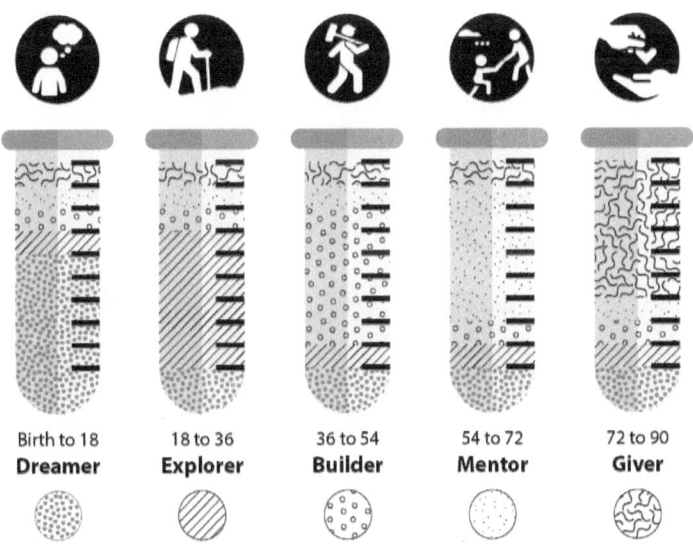

FIGURE 2: THE PRINCIPLE OF 18 IN ACTION

| Birth to 18 | 18 to 36 | 36 to 54 | 54 to 72 | 72 to 90 |
| Dreamer | Explorer | Builder | Mentor | Giver |

It's important at this point to note that the Principle of 18 is not a comprehensive how-to book for all areas of personal development—you'll want to seek targeted advice for skills like goal-setting, financial literacy, and mentoring, for example. This book is a wake-up call that presents an integrated approach to a unique and fulfilling life. Its strength is in its unified, high-level approach to viewing your life.

If you think of your life on this Earth as a journey of self-discovery, where you navigate the river of life at your speed, the Principle of 18 shows you how to reinvent yourself at five critical intervals. As the old proverb says, "No matter how long you've been traveling on the wrong road, turn back." You may think you're stuck, but you are not. No matter where you are now, you know more than you did when you started out, which means that if you start using this system to change your life, you'll be ahead of the game!

THE DREAMER
Imagining Your Future
— Childhood to 18 —

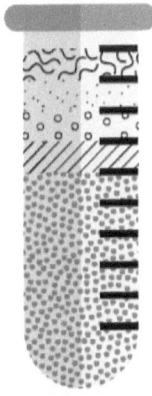

Birth to 18
Dreamer

"So many of our dreams at first seem impossible, then seem improbable, and then, when we summon the will, they soon seem inevitable."
—Christopher Reeve

NORTH STAR

It's scary to think about trying to realize your dreams, especially when they're big ones. Would you even be able to get there? What kind of a person you would be if you *did* realize your dreams? Would you still have the same friends? Live in the same area? No doubt, any worthwhile dream will change you in the process of coming true. But your daring and out-there dreams are the rocket fuel that will propel you forward.

To live an extraordinary life, you must have big, bold dreams. That is the first step. The second step is to overcome your fears. We all have fears, and we all need to face them to move forward. The poet Rilke wrote that "Our deepest fears are like dragons guarding our deepest treasure." What will you find in the dark cave that the dragon is guarding—a pot of gold, or an empty bag? Will you even come out alive from the encounter?

You will *never* know until you sharpen your sword and slay the dragon. It's easier to look at a mighty dragon on a foggy mountain ledge in front of a mysterious cave and say to yourself, "I think I'll pass on this one. Maybe next time I'm in the area the dragon won't be here, and I can just climb up to the cave and take what's mine." But the dragon will always be there. To realize who you truly are, you will need to fight. Fighting the dragon is the only way to move forward, grow, and develop. It's not an easy task. Slaying dragons is a nasty, sweaty, bloody business. But if you prevail—and there *is* a good chance you'll prevail—you'll enter the cave knowing you faced your terrors and lived to tell the tale.

Life is there for the taking, but first, you must dream it.

The most important thing at the beginning of this journey is to believe that your dreams will come true, and know that they're not idle fantasies or vacant daydreams. They might seem too big given your current circumstances, but even your boldest dreams can come true—believe me. Who would have thought, back when I was a kid from a shattered family in Tel Aviv, that I would be able to command the attention of the world's top executives from companies such as Amazon, Xerox, Verizon, HP, Dell, and Bank of New York Mellon? I had big dreams for myself, and even though it took many years, I eventually realized them. And when dreams come true, it's one of the best feelings in the world!

We all start at square one. Cultivating dreams that can move you is like planting acorns, tending to them, watering them, and watching them grow. Most will not grow at all, for whatever reason. Some will grow but not reach their full potential. A few—the special ones—will reach for the stars. Your dreams need that sense of unlimited possibility. They need to excite you; make you wake up early in the morning with anticipation to see where this journey will take you.

The Dreamer

Most young people do not have big dreams or a compelling vision for their future. During my coaching sessions, I find that quite often their dreams are blurry. Low-definition. They miss critical elements and rarely represent the Dreamer's true potential.

Why is it crucial that you start thinking about your purpose in life at such an early age? Why not go with the flow and see where life will take you? You can certainly take that approach, and you could very well find what you are looking for by stumbling along and figuring things out as they happen to you.

On the other hand, you might not. And this is your life we are talking about here! You only get one shot, so why not give it your all? As a Dreamer, you should be learning about your dreams, finding the right Mentors, and thinking about specific steps to realize your aspirations—but not actually following through and trying to reach them. That belongs in the Explorer stage, when you'll try out your dreams and discover whether they'll prepare you for your Builder phase. Then you'll double your efforts for 18 years before switching gears and beginning to give back.

When we leave major life decisions to fate, they can end in vastly different ways than we'd hoped. That's why having a grand plan for your entire life makes so much sense. Now, planning your life doesn't mean surprises won't arise or that you'll get exactly where you need to be. Luck will play a significant role, like it or not, but any efforts to set deliberate intentions and take decisive actions will go a long way toward getting you where you need to be. If you don't have a plan, someone else will have a plan for you. By dreaming up the best version of yourself, you can give yourself the best chance at the success *you* want and deserve.

Backyard Blues

My life was characterized by uncertainty from an early age. When I was two years old, my father was severely wounded, suffering a major head trauma. I was too young to remember or understand all that went on around me, but the trajectory of our family changed in a profound way. Growing up in this environment with a volatile father who alternated between shows of affection and tyrannical mood swings was not for the faint of heart.

My father believed in strict discipline. I had to wake up every day at the crack of dawn, rain or shine, and *do something*. It didn't matter what, as long as I was working from the first light of day. I resented those early mornings, trudging out of my warm bed to complete meaningless chores in our neglected backyard, which never showed signs of improvement. Water is scarce in Israel, so my father watered the lawn only once a week; in that arid climate, trying to maintain any sort of growth was a hopeless endeavor.

Our house resembled a military boot camp: early morning wake-ups, manual labor before school, two-minute cold showers, food rations, manual labor after school. Rinse and repeat. Once when I was nine years old, I fell on a metal sprinkler and injured my knee while playing soccer with my friends. I was terrified by the blood streaming down my leg. The older kids helped me to my feet and carried me to our house, where my father was watering the plants outside. When he saw the

The Dreamer

commotion, he asked all the kids to leave, then continued to water the plants. I approached him and said in a shaken voice,

"I got hurt playing soccer..."

My father continued to water the dry yellow grass. I started crying in pain and disbelief. After several minutes he turned to me, the green hose still in his hand. He glanced at the bloody knee, nodded, and said, raising two fingers, "There are two basic conditions in life. Either you are dead, or you are alive." He folded one finger down. "If you are dead, there is nothing to be done about it." He moved the finger from side to side dismissively to denote the finality of this condition, then raised the other finger. "If you are alive, learn to shut up and carry on without complaining." He headed inside.

I shouted in confusion, "What should I do?"

Without turning around, my father said, "Just wash it with water. It's nothing, only skin deep." He closed the door behind him. I knelt to inspect my knee; the white bone was clearly visible. I fainted right then and there. Luckily, a neighbor saw me slumped next to the water hose, picked me up, and drove me to the emergency room. A couple of tetanus shots and fifteen stitches later, he took me home. My mother was beside herself with worry. My father was watching soccer on TV and didn't give me a second look.

What I didn't realize at the time was that my father's intention was not to hurt, but to make sure I could cope with whatever life threw at me. He was dealt a harsh hand at the height of his powers, and wanted to prepare me for the hardships that lay ahead. Most young kids would not understand this approach; I know I didn't. I just got angry at having to wake up so early to do chores that didn't yield any measurable results. My mother tried to protect me, but she was often powerless against my father.

Years passed, brutally scorching summers followed by cold, bitter winters. The backyard looked the same: yellow grass mixed with weeds, bare spots where the grass didn't take hold, a thorny bush that kept piercing my skin. I had started to dream about escaping my life in Tel Aviv and moving to the United States. But I was only a young boy; there was no way I could accomplish such a dramatic move at that age. I kept dreaming, and started to look to books and movies for inspiration about how to overcome difficult situations. One of these movies left a particularly strong impression on me.

Escape from Devil's Island

When I was twelve years old, I watched *Papillon*. *Papillon* is the story of a French prisoner by the name of Henri Charrière (played by Steve McQueen) who is serving a life sentence at Devil's Island, a notoriously brutal prison island off the coast of French Guiana in South America. The place reeks of desperation; it's a shark-infested pile of rocks in the middle of the Atlantic Ocean. The last scene made a profound impact on me back then; even now, it manages to move me.

Henri stares at the infinite blue ocean from an enormous cliff on Devil's Island. There are no guards around, since no one has ever escaped from this desolate, godforsaken place. Huge waves break powerfully on the cliff's lofty walls, roaring like an animal detecting easy prey. Henri, who has never given up on his hope of becoming a free man, now has white hair. Some of his teeth are missing, and his eyesight is weak from long stays in the dungeon. His only friend, Louis Dega (played

The Dreamer

by Dustin Hoffman), has accepted the fact that he will die on this lonely cliff in the middle of the ocean, but Henri has a different plan.

After a lengthy period of observation, Henri is convinced they can escape by jumping off the cliff into the ocean, then drifting to shore on jute bags filled with coconuts. He somehow manages to convince his old friend to join him in this last adventure.

They stand together on the mighty cliff, looking down at the raging ocean, making their final reckoning. The wind blows furiously around them. Henri throws down his bag of coconuts and the bag makes its long, slow, arcing way to the wild waves. Louis watches the bag's flight, reflecting on the arc of his own life.

Even before the bag touches the waves, he understands that he will not be able to join his good friend. This adventure is too big for him. He has come to terms with his fate, and a dramatic jump into the unknown is not something that he, or any other ordinary person, would ever consider.

But Henri is not an ordinary person. His long years spent in unbearable conditions, and the cruel penalties he has suffered for every failed escape, have only made him more determined to be a free man. Physically he is but a shadow of his former self, a ghost of the healthy, robust man he used to be. But mentally he is ridiculously strong, and ready to make his dream come true. He embraces Louis for the last time, smiles at him toothlessly, and jumps off the cliff.

He floats in the air in a leap that seems to last forever.

He disappears in the raging waves—until we see him swimming toward the coconut bag. With enormous effort, he manages to swim away from the narrow bay, and as the camera zooms in for a close-up, we hear him scream, "I'm still here, you bastards!"

This is the victory of the human spirit: a heroic struggle to win back one's freedom. This movie had a profound influence on me back then, as the themes of overcoming incredible odds and never giving up echoed in my own life. In high school, my number-one dream was to build a new life for myself—somewhere far away, where I could start from scratch on my own terms, complete with a house that would have a green and healthy backyard. When I finally came to the United States at the age of twenty-one after my military service in Israel, I had no connections, no family, and limited resources. I embodied your classic immigrant story.

I could have stayed in Israel and started my life there, surrounded by friends and family. That was the safe and known path. But it was not *my* path. I wanted to experience a different culture in a faraway place, to struggle to learn a new language, and to find out if I could fit in and make it work. My dream was to throw myself into unfamiliar territory and make it on my own. Granted, this is not a survival story; I was not parachuted into a jungle in South America and made to survive. But it was a dream that I'd cultivated for a long time—a sort of a test, if you will. It took me six years to realize that I could achieve it, until I was twenty-seven.

Dream Killers

Some of the advice from those who are close to you will ring true. When we feel like someone "gets it," we are open to receiving and acting on their suggestions. But many people's

The Dreamer

advice will be thinly veiled criticisms of your ambitions. Ask yourself if the person talking to you understands your unique position—your hopes and fears. You need people in your corner who believe in you, and you must learn the difference between Dream Killers and Mentors.

Dream killers quickly become easy to spot. For example, when you tell them your dream is to perform on Broadway, or that you would like to build a network of like-minded Dreamers, or that you want to become a professional musician—*big dreams*—they will respond with "That will never happen in a million years," or "Forget about it. Those dreams will just break your heart." Or they'll give you the worst kind of response: a condescending look or smile, and maybe a head shake to indicate your stupidity. Keep your dreams to yourself if you suspect the person you're speaking to is a dream killer, and learn to trust only those people that push you forward towards realizing your aspirations.

Use your intuition—becoming more intuitive will serve you well in all areas of life. Albert Einstein said, "The only real valuable thing is intuition." Steve Jobs commented that "Intuition is an immensely powerful thing. More powerful than intellect, in my opinion."

But what *is* intuition, and how do you use it? It's difficult to define, but it has many names: a gut feeling, a hunch, a nudge, an instinct. It's something inside you that tells you what's going on around you, who to trust and who to avoid. To be effective, you must learn to trust your intuition and act on it, even if you can't rationally explain it. Intuition truly is "just a feeling."

The next time you listen to someone, don't just listen to their words; see what kind of feelings arise in you and what your body tells you about them. We all have this gift, but somehow we forget to use it—or we just don't trust ourselves. Expressions such as "sniffing someone out" or "getting a feel for someone" all hint at the same thing: figuring out the essence of the person in front of you. Are they trustworthy? Are they looking at your best interests? Should you heed their advice, or take whatever they tell you with a grain of salt?

I know that when I trust my intuition I make better decisions, even if I can't explain exactly what is happening. And whenever I choose to suppress or ignore what that little voice tells me, I pay the price.

It is beyond me why the world is filled with so many dream killers. My take is that most of them are trying to help in a twisted kind of way by shielding you from life's harsh realities. Chances are they tried to achieve one of *their* dreams and it didn't work out.

When a dream killer is your best friend or a member of your family, proceed with caution. If the people who are closest to you are not supportive of your dreams, it might be best to keep your aspirations to yourself until you can start realizing them.

How to Dream

Your focus should be on fleshing out your dreams, creating detailed maps that lead to realizing them. Focus on the process, not the outcome or result. That's the key to creating a vision with a serious shot at becoming a reality.

For example, if your dream is to become a national trial lawyer and all you do is imagine yourself dazzling the jury and the judge on prime-time TV, you are not helping yourself get there. You need to think about the specific steps between

The Dreamer

here and there and visualize yourself taking each one. Talk to trial attorneys and find out which paths they have taken, which steps got them to where they are today. Maybe there are only ten steps, or maybe there are twenty or thirty. Once you know, you can visualize a staircase where each step represents a milestone.

Consider another example: a sixth-grade girl who dreams of becoming a Broadway actor. Will it help if all she does is fantasize about her debut as the star? It would be more effective to show her the important milestones she needs to reach. You could help her draw a treasure map that marks the challenges she'll need to overcome, from acting in middle school and high school productions, to taking singing lessons, going to shows, auditioning for summer stock, and so on. Each treasure she unearths is a step closer to her dream.

When you move into the Explorer stage, concentrate on only the next three or four steps on the staircase—no more. You want to make a small progress each day. After completing a few steps, move on to the next set without thinking about the final destination. Thinking about your final goal will just distract you from your daily progress, especially if it's a big goal. The advice so many people dish out—just picture yourself in your ideal future, and you'll magically make it there—is unrealistic. You need to envision every step and plan for the next milestone.

Outline the entire process, even if your dream will take years to realize, and think about how you will get there, step by step. You could use a journal, a whiteboard, or Post-It notes to capture all these steps. Following this step-by-step process will give you a significant advantage: it prompts you to make deliberate choices about how you want to live your life. You'll build confidence in your ability to not only design your ideal life, but also to make it happen when the time comes for exploring these dreams. This is the rocket fuel that will propel you forward.

When we see things in our minds—especially when we see them repeatedly and in detail—it can begin to seem like they are real. It can also inspire us to take the necessary actions to make that imaginary future come true. Dreaming about that amazing trip to France over and over—smelling the croissants, tasting the wine, hearing the French accent—might lead you to starting to plan an actual trip. How much are the flights? Where are the best places to visit? If we dream about something long enough, we just might convince ourselves that it is reality, then go about making that reality happen. Many studies have shown that people who deliberately imagine specific events rate them as more likely to occur than people who have not imagined them.

Research in the field of sport psychology indicates that specific methods can increase our success with this technique. Researchers have found that process simulation is a powerful way to imagine the real-life steps required to reach our goals. If your dream is to attend a prestigious culinary institute so you can become a successful chef one day, you would do well to imagine the steps required to get there. You could imagine yourself researching top culinary institutes, gathering information about the application process, deciding which institutes to apply to, and completing applications. You are not doing all these steps in real life yet; you're just thinking through each one in detail. Simply *imagining* taking each of

The Dreamer

these important steps increases the likelihood that you will carry out these tasks and secure a real-life admission to the culinary institute of your dreams.

Why is this approach so effective? By repeating the steps required to reach a goal, even just in our heads, we force ourselves to walk through them and come up with a plan we can implement in real life. As we undergo this mental process, we often experience positive emotions that motivate us to create momentum in real life. All of this is vital when it comes to realizing our goals.

Another approach is to actively focus on the result you hope to realize, rather than on the process that will get you there. You might imagine that you are a scuba instructor or an international interpreter, or see yourself living in a big mansion in upstate New York or sailing a yacht in the Bahamas. Outcome simulation requires that we envision ourselves already there, actively carrying out our roles or desires. Supporters of this approach claim that our simulated experience of actively fulfilling our dreams increases our motivation, prompting behaviors that will lead to the desired outcomes.

I recommend combining the two approaches, but not equally. Spend eighty percent of your time thinking about the specific steps that will get you there, and twenty percent imagining that you are already there. If you spend most of your time just imagining the result without considering the steps needed to get there, you'll be less likely to get started and move along the path of your dream. In fact, a group of researchers at UCLA studied a specific type of outcome simulation—wishful thinking—and found that it may be *detrimental* to achieving goals. Their findings showed that students who used process simulation before their midterm exams scored significantly higher than those who relied on outcome simulation. The people who used process simulation were more engaged in planning, problem-solving, and using effective emotion-regulation strategies. On the other hand, students who engaged in wishful thinking–type outcome simulation by hoping the exam would be unbelievably easy were less likely to use active problem-solving strategies and reported fewer positive results compared to those who focused on the steps needed to succeed in the exam.

Another powerful technique is daydreaming—and yes, daydreaming can truly be considered a technique! All of us have let our minds wander without realizing the benefits of doing so: staring out the window, dreaming of another world, imagining another time or place. People tend to view daydreaming as a problematic behavior or something to avoid, but it allows us to engage in a world that is unburdened by external demands and limitations. It offers us a priceless opportunity to connect to our creative side. As J.R.R. Tolkien wrote in *The Lord of the Rings*, "Not all those who wander are lost." I like to think this refers to mental wandering as well as physical, since a wandering mind can often find creative solutions that would escape the logical mind. To become the Dreamer, you will need to learn how to dream, and daydreaming is a perfect place to start.

Researchers have found that we spend half our waking hours engaged in daydreaming. Many people try to avoid it or snap out of it, thinking it's unproductive or a waste of time. But daydreaming is associated with positive outcomes that contribute to success, including innovation, exploration,

The Dreamer

a greater sense of self, creativity, and relaxation. In fact, many well-known, successful people were noted daydreamers—individuals like Albert Einstein, Isaac Newton, and the Greek mathematician Archimedes. There seems to be a strong link between daydreaming and creativity.

Daydreaming is one of the key attributes of highly creative people and is crucial to the development and expression of original ideas. It improves critical thinking and problem-solving by linking the parts of our brain dedicated to analysis and execution with the parts of our brain that engage in higher-level thinking. Multiple studies have shown that people who daydream perform better on tests of creative thinking than those who do not.

The important thing to note is *how* we daydream, since it has a significant impact on the outcomes that you are looking for. People who engage in positive daydreaming, where they see themselves happy and successful in various challenging scenarios along an arduous journey, tend to be more open to experiences and ideas, more in touch with their imaginative side, and more responsive to their sensations and feelings. Positive daydreaming strengthens these qualities and sets us up for richer experiences, better moods, and enhanced creativity.

On the other hand, people who engage in negative daydreaming are more likely to experience higher levels of depression, so it is important to pay attention to the type of daydreaming you do. If your daydreaming is filled with anxieties and worries (What if people laugh at my speech tonight? What if I say the wrong thing on that first date that I am so excited about?), it will not be productive. On the other hand, if your daydreams are filled with excitement about the future, imagining what could go right and all the steps needed to achieve positive outcomes, you are more likely to experience success and happiness. Daydreaming about goals, aspirations, dreams, and what you need to do to achieve them can notably increase your chances of success.

One researcher, E. Paul Torrance, discovered the positive impact of daydreaming by following a group of children from elementary school into adulthood. He attempted to predict the subjects' achievements through a wide variety of measures, including grades and IQ tests, and found that the kids who had daydreamed the most about who they would be as an adult were the most successful later in life.

Slowing down, interrupting the daily grind, thinking things over, and allowing your mind to wander freely through ideas and goal-oriented fantasies are all important steps in understanding what is going in with your life. Taking the time to let your mind wander is well worth it, because the journey brings about valuable "Aha!" moments that provide important insights and new perspectives.

How many dreams should you have?

There are benefits to having one big dream and thinking day and night about how to make it come true, but there are also several significant risks. During the Dreamer stage, you are too young to limit yourself to one dream that may or may not work. In your first 18 years, I encourage you to develop several dreams for your future.

It's important to realize that when you will be in the Explorer stage, you might come up with a completely new dream! Life is dynamic and ever-changing, and you might learn or

The Dreamer

experience something that changes your entire worldview. However, the work you'll need to do as an Explorer will force you to think long and hard about what it takes to realize a particular dream. What are the specific steps? Who can help you along the way? Which challenges will you face?

All these elements are part of the dream-creation process. Even if you ditch all or some of your dreams as you grow older, the work you invest in thinking about your original dreams will come in handy: you'll already have a proven process. And who knows? Maybe you'll get a chance to live out your early dreams at a later stage in life when you have the means, time, or experience that you lacked when you were younger!

Your dreams don't have to be completely different from each other. If you love horses above everything else, one of your dreams could be riding competitively; another might be learning how to become a breeder; and yet another could be learning how to use horses for therapeutic reasons, such as working with children who have emotional issues. The love of horses unites all these dreams, even though each one would take you on a different path.

However, you will often have different visions for your future. Imagine wanting to pursue these distinct dreams:

- Becoming a science fiction author
- Becoming a professional surfer
- Becoming a trader on Wall Street

These are vastly different dreams. Each one would take you on a different path, and each one would take years to pursue. If you want to become a writer, you could go to college and get a degree in literature, philosophy, or history while you continue writing and practicing your trade. You could also skip college and take a creative writing class. Or you could just start writing with no formal training. Either way, it will take time—even years—before you can see whether your dream of becoming a writer will work out for you. The path to publishing is a treacherous road that requires a unique set of skills, from finding an agent to marketing your books, and you'll learn them the hard way, with massive effort at each step.

If you want to become a pro surfer, you'll have to compete with the most talented surfers in the world, just as any elite athlete does. Assuming you're a talented surfer to begin with, the road to becoming a pro is a tremendously difficult endeavor that requires intense training, focus, and dedication. It will take years to see whether this plan pans out.

You might ask yourself why you can't pursue both dreams at the same time by surfing every morning and writing in the evenings. I wish you could, but things don't usually work that way.

A good example of the need to focus on one dream at a time can be found in the Japanese novelist Haruki Murakami. In his twenties, right after college, he started a small jazz club in Tokyo. His friends and family predicted that he would fail miserably since he had no business experience, but he took out a sizable loan, opened the jazz club, and ran it successfully. This was his first dream, and he stayed with it for ten years, until he was thirty. Then he paused and took stock of his path up to that moment in time. His other dream was to become a novelist, and he realized that if he wanted to take a serious stab at it, this was the time to do it. He convinced his wife to sell the jazz club and pay back the loan so he could dedicate himself to writing.

The Dreamer

Quite surprisingly for someone as young as he was, Murakami realized that he needed to give himself full permission to pursue his dream. He did not try to run the jazz club at night and write in the morning. A halfhearted effort simply would not do; he'd have to give it all he had. Murakami pursued two dreams in his Explorer stage, and he struck gold the second time. He went for it and immersed himself in trying to make it work. Only after you have done the same will you know whether you've gone far enough.

Our third hypothetical scenario of becoming a trader on Wall Street, also requires a major investment of time and effort. You need a college degree, preferably in finance or business, and to work hard at applying to banks and brokerage firms. When you arrive on the trading floor, you'll start in a junior position, helping senior traders with research and support. It will take you several years to find out if you're good at trading and enjoy its high-pressure environment.

When I tell young people in the Dreamer stage about the need to produce several dreams, as well as the detailed processes that will make them come true, they often ask "How do I know which dream to pursue first?" This is easy. Your passion and enthusiasm will show you the way.

Let's assume you decide becoming a trader on Wall Street is your top dream. In your Explorer stage, you should go for it—full steam ahead. Then after you've done it for several years, stop to reassess whether it's what you want to do as a Builder, between the ages of 36 to 54, or whether it's time to try on another dream.

How many dreams should you cultivate for your future as a Dreamer? My recommendation is three—no more and no less. When you move on to the next phase, the Explorer, you will have enough time to explore all three.

Why not explore ten or twenty, you might be wondering. You'll find the following sentence incredibly hard to believe, but even with the generous allowance of 18 years dedicated to exploration, **you will run out of time**. Exploring takes time, dedication, effort, and the ability to immerse yourself in your dream. Nothing worthwhile is easily achieved, but your unique combination of talents, passion, and personality will take you as far as you are willing to go.

You have nothing to prove as a Dreamer or Explorer—that's part of the beauty of those stages. When you become a Builder in your mid-thirties, *that's* when things get serious; that is when you have 18 years to build whatever you need to build. The pressure you put on yourself as a Dreamer and Explorer is internal.

It will take several years to manifest your dreams in the real world. If you absolutely love the outdoors and your dream is to become a forest ranger, it will take a few years to get good at what you do before you can decide whether you want to explore another dream. Some people find their destiny in pursuit of their first dream, but most of us must explore until we find the groove that leads us into the Builder phase. Many times, we end up pasting together bits and pieces from our original three dreams to explore another dream that leads to our life's work.

If you feel utterly miserable from the get-go, move on. Certain dreams will immediately crash on the hard rock of reality, and you might realize that they're just not for you. There's

The Dreamer

nothing wrong with that. It's just part of the learning process, and it will help you narrow down what *is* right for you.

One of my early dreams was to become a veterinarian, but after spending time with actual vets and seeing the guts and glory of it all, I quickly changed my mind. Revelations like that can be disappointing, but you must pick yourself up and move on to your next dream when it happens.

The start of anything is going to be difficult. You'll be assigned the most mundane, repetitive, boring tasks. You won't be able to enjoy the perks of your target position. You'll put in long hours and long days. All this is to be expected. But if you feel in your bones that you've made a grave mistake, give serious consideration to why you feel like that. If you realize that this dream is not for you, move on to the next one.

It is quite possible that your top three dreams will change between your Dreamer and Explorer stages. Maybe you'll have better information after pursuing one dream. Maybe you'll meet someone you trust who tells you not to take that path. Perhaps something more enticing comes along, a brand-new dream that seizes you with power and wonder. You might ask, given the highly dynamic nature of life, why you need to invest in fully exploring three dreams during your Explorer years. Why can't you change your mind a million times and see where you end up?

These are good questions, and they have a good answer. When you wholeheartedly pursue a dream you've imagined fully, you'll feel a spark that makes you want to get out of bed in the morning. Even if it turns out that a dream is not for you, the magic is in the process you develop: your own method of tackling a dream, wrestling it to the ground, and finding out if it's the right future for you.

Exploring each dream will take several years, and you will learn valuable lessons along the way. Chief among them is *how* to explore your dreams: what it takes to get there, what kind of commitment you need, what kind of mindset will help you see it through.

If one of your dreams is to become a rapper, going through the process of producing your songs, marketing them, and immersing yourself in the music world will teach you valuable lessons about patience, tenacity, and confidence. Even if you decide after a few years that you can't break through, you will have gained an appreciation of what it takes to realize your ambitions. When you start to pursue your next dream, you'll already know how to go about it.

But if all you do is jump from one thing to the other without fully immersing yourself in one dream at a time, you will never realize what it takes to carry an ambition to its full potential. You will only have a superficial knowledge of how to make things work in your favor. Even if it takes several years, seeing things through is the best course of action.

Each time you go through a full cycle of dream realization, you'll get better at it. You'll be better able to figure out which resources you need, who you need in your corner, what mindset you need to develop, how to think long term, which strategies work for you, and what challenges or obstacles you must overcome. By following this process, you develop your mental muscles—a resilience that will serve you well when you decide on your ultimate path.

The Dreamer

I realize that it's challenging to commit to your top dream without knowing whether it will work out. I wish there was a way to predict the future, but there's no magic formula or crystal ball. You must commit to the experiment anyway. Think long and hard about what excites you, what are you uniquely good at, and what skills you'd enjoy developing. Find the sweet spot between your interests, skills, aptitudes, and passion. You have enough time on your hands in the 18 years of your Explorer phase to try out three dreams in a meaningful way. Think of it as three opportunities to strike gold. Fulfill the promise of each dream, and you will be on a solid path to success.

What happens if you dedicate a few years to each dream and reach the conclusion that what you really want to do is completely different—a fourth dream, perhaps? There is no problem at all here. You have not wasted your life by living out the three dreams you thought would make you happy and fulfilled. Remember that one of the central ideas of "The Principle of 18" is to minimize regrets. You tried living your dreams and then realized that it's something else that draws you in. Go for it full force. This fourth dream could hold the key to your future.

The Right Mentor

The challenge with big dreams is that you cannot achieve them on your own; you need a guide that will help show you the way. A critical objective during your Dreamer and Explorer stages is to find a suitable Mentor—or even better, Mentors—and follow their lead. These Mentors see your potential, believe in you, and realize you're young. They understand that it will take a long time for you to blossom and fulfill your dreams. The best Mentors take an active part in your journey by offering encouragement, providing personal connections to their network, and recommending great resources that can inspire you to act.

How do you pick the right Mentor? First, don't make the mistake of aiming too high. This might sound strange, but most people have an inflated sense of what an ideal Mentor should be, and they fail to develop meaningful relationships with someone more accessible.

When I was a college student I idolized Michael Jordan, but whenever I tried his moves on the court, it ended badly. Having someone to look up to and emulate is beneficial, but an extraordinary role model may hurt us in the long run. They might make us feel deflated rather than inspired when we look to them. There are a few reasons for this.

1) If the people we look up to are exceptionally outstanding, we may feel like their achievements are impossible for us to attain. One study that examined the impact of role models on feelings of self-worth found that women who were shown super-achieving female leaders reported greater feelings of inferiority than women who were shown less-accomplished role models.

2) Not everyone at a high point in their industry has gotten there in ways you'd want to emulate. Some worked obsessively, day and night, ignoring their relationships. Some took unseemly detours that would compromise your values. Some had advantages that you simply do not possess.

3) One important quality of a role model is the ability to guide others effectively and empathetically. Many people who have achieved extraordinary success find it difficult to understand other people's struggles.

We will do better by choosing role models who consistently perform well, rather than those at the very top of their fields. Consider this example from the world of surfing.

Kelly Slater is the best surfer of all time. He has won eleven world championships and is simultaneously the youngest *and* the oldest ever world champion. If you want to become a professional surfer, looking to Kelly Slater as a role model would be a total waste of your time. His skills and accomplishments are out of this world, and if you compare yourself to him, you will come up painfully short, no matter how long you train or compete.

A more sensible approach would be to develop a local relationship with a top surfer in your community, someone you can see and talk to every day. They might not have accomplished what Kelly Slater has, but if you're lucky, they will teach you how to get to the next level. They will become a source of inspiration for you—and not just in the water.

Massively successful people are often willing to live with enormous amounts of stress. A friend of mine who runs a thriving business in Los Angeles looks from the outside like he has all the success symbols: the red Ferrari, the beach house, membership in a fancy country club. But when you know he spends most of his time in court suing or getting sued by his competitors, you might ask whether it's worth it. He's willing to pay the price and live with this constant pressure, but are you? Are you willing to sacrifice that much? Are you willing to take on all that stress? What is the ideal work-life balance for you?

If financial success is extremely important to you, you can get there, but I don't recommend cultivating a single-minded focus on getting rich. Sure, if you're willing to sacrifice your personal life and your important relationships, and if you can push yourself to work hard every single day, you will get rich, no doubt. But at what cost?

Don't try to follow the super-successful. Seek out Mentors who have a solid record in your area of interest. The path they took should be visible to you—don't believe any overnight-success stories or people whose path is needlessly obscure.

The Interviews

Your Mentor will be there for support and guidance, but one of the best ways to learn about your dreams is to interview people who live and breathe them every day. Look for people who are doing exactly what you want to do. If your dream is to become a veterinarian, go out and interview vets in your area. You might be surprised at how willing people are to help you out.

Keep a couple of things in mind as you set about interviewing people in your chosen field. First, allow time for scheduling. Don't call today and expect to come in tomorrow. Depending on how busy someone is, you might ask for a meeting a month or even several months out. Specify that you need thirty minutes and keep to it. Prepare a list of questions for the interview and feel free to send it ahead of time. You might even get to shadow this person for an afternoon; you never know.

The Dreamer

Try to interview three people in the role you seek and ask them the same questions. Get a feel for what it's like to be do that work on a daily basis. A few potential questions:

- What made you choose this profession?
- What's great about what you do? What *don't* you like about this profession?
- What turned out to be different from your expectations?
- What about the business side of it—how difficult is it?
- What kind of skills do I need to succeed in this profession? What mindset?
- If you could go back twenty years, would you still pursue this career? Would you do anything differently?

Transition Plan: From Dreamer to Explorer

Your dreams about your future should get you so excited that you cannot wait to try them out, to see what it would be like to live that kind of life. They should be something that propel you from your bed early in the morning and delight you for the rest of the day as you think about them. To do that, a dream must be big and bold!

Goethe said, "Dream no small dreams for they have no power to move the hearts of men." A great dream needs a sense of wonder; something unexpected and unique. If your dream doesn't fit that description, I suggest coming up with a new one.

While you're in the Dreamer stage, keep a dream journal nearby for your thoughts, processes, resources, connections, and questions. Write down everything that could help you in your Explorer stage.

Things outside of your control will always happen, but they should not stop you from planning for the future, experimenting, taking risks, and becoming who you need to be. The only way to start is to dream about who you want to become and the specific steps that will get you where you need to be.

The Dreamer phase, to age 18, provides a container for your aspirations—a place where you can visualize who you could become. In the Explorer phase, from 18 to 36, you will find out whether your dreams are aligned with who you want to be and whether you have the skills and motivation you need to realize your vision. In the Builder stage, from 36 to 54, you'll have time to achieve mastery in your chosen area and realize the full potential of your dreams.

There are people out there who are exploring your dream right now, and you're in the fortunate position of being able to learn from their explorations. To find out what's working and what isn't and adapt accordingly. If you want perspective on what is tremendously important in life, interview Builders (36 to 54), Mentors (54 to 72) and even Givers (over 72). You can learn from people in each stage. Explorers will provide the most immediate and relevant connections because they are trying out their dreams in real time. Builders are difficult to engage because they're busy laying the foundation for their future. Mentors will be able to share the hard-won knowledge that came from years of experience. Givers can offer their time and attention, coupled with an unparalleled ability to look at the big picture, at the entire arc of your life's journey.

Every one of us has a unique ability to plan, organize, strategize, and effect change in our own life. We can conceptualize where we are now, where we want to be in the future, and what steps will bridge the two. With three fully formed dreams, complete with the steps that would make them come true, you will have a clear path to follow into your Explorer life stage.

Key Ideas for Dreamers

Identify three compelling dreams for your future. You need a high-definition vision for your future, even if you end up doing something radically different than you originally thought you would. These dreams must be detailed and specific and include all the steps required to realize them.

Use visualization to your advantage. You can do this by mixing positive daydreaming, outcome simulation, and process simulation, with a bias toward process and steps.

Interview role models. Find several people who are doing what you want to do. Interview them, then incorporate what you learn into your dream mapping.

Find and work with the right mentor. Learn from someone who has been there before you and can show you what's around the corner, what to focus on, and what to avoid. Don't reach out to super-successful people, but rather to those you respect and who are willing to guide you on your journey. As a young Dreamer, you should be able to find a Mentor who will not charge you for their time.

Beware of dream killers. Your dreams are a precious part of who you are and who you want to be. Shy away from dream killers by not sharing your hopes and aspirations with them.

THE EXPLORER
The Adventure Begins

—————— *18 to 36* ——————

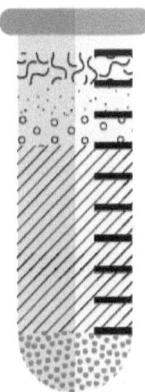

18 to 36
Explorer

"Success is never final, and failure is seldom fatal. It's courage that counts."
—Winston Churchill

NORTH STAR

When I look at how most people in the Dreamer and Explorer stages of their lives view their work years, I get depressed. Many of the young people I coach subscribe to a version of the following plan: "After college or learning a trade, I'll get a job, then work for the next forty years, and when I get to my late sixties or early seventies, I'll retire."

According to the National Institute on Retirement Security, sixty-five percent of American households are at risk of not making it financially in the retirement years. That means that all these years of mind-numbing, demanding work and sacrifices *still* do not guarantee safe passage into retirement. What is wrong with this picture? Where is the joy in following such a bleak plan for most of your life?

Hard work is part and parcel of the work ethos, and without it nothing meaningful will happen, no matter what field you are in. But hard work without a plan—without playing to your strengths and taking advantage of situations as they arise—will only get you so far. The prospect of working hard for forty years straight toward an uncertain outcome doesn't sound attractive. Besides, if that's the main route to success, why are so many people missing out on the American Dream?

The simple answer is that you cannot work for that long and keep your spark alive. Your body will tire, your spirit will despair. There are a few exceptions, like highly motivated entrepreneurs and ridiculously gifted artists. But most people are not trying to set a course for their entire life, and many of us just get it *wrong*. Very few people question the "common knowledge" that your working years should start in your mid-twenties and end forty years later, in your mid-sixties—all without a break, at the same pace and intensity, year after year without fail.

Think about it: Do we expect anything else to run for forty consecutive years at peak performance? Can you imagine an athlete running a marathon every single day? Nature doesn't work like that. We have bursts of energy and growth, then periods of lull and recovery. We are awake for sixteen hours at a time, then need to rest for eight hours. Some people get away with less sleep, but even they need a lull period. Yet common wisdom dictates that we need to show up for work every single day and keep our energy, focus, creativity, and stamina at the same levels for years at a time. We think we can compensate for these long stretches of work by taking occasional vacations, but the truth is that they are rarely long enough, and it's exceedingly difficult to unplug.

When I was in my early thirties, my wife and I decided to sell all our possessions and embark on a one-year journey around the world. I wouldn't call it a vacation, but it's what we needed to get away from it all. It wasn't easy to decide to leave

The Explorer

everything—including our careers—behind, but it was one of my best decisions. You can read about it in my book, *Before the Kids and Mortgage*.

Most people get into the rat race and then slog through life, lost in the daily grind, trying to keep their heads above water. But research has consistently shown that most employees are not engaged in their work; they just don't care. Companies spend billions of dollars trying to ramp up productivity and increase morale, commitment, and engagement, but nothing seems to work. And why *would* it? If you were in your twenties, looking down the road at a bleak forty-year slog, how motivated would *you* be?

There is another way to look at your life. If you spend your twenties and thirties exploring until you find the one area at which you can excel, where you can really make a difference, you can work at it from your mid-thirties to mid-fifties, honing your skills, becoming adept at whatever you've set your sights on. And you can do it while having fun and not taking yourself too seriously, because you know you're making daily progress toward your goals. Even baby steps forward will work in your favor since you are using the rule of compound interest to advance your life.

With compound interest, even tiny daily changes yield fantastic results over the years. If you were given one penny and then doubled it every day for a month, you would end up with the unbelievable amount of $10 million. This is the power of compounding your efforts every single day. Albert Einstein called compound interest "the eighth wonder of the world. He who understands it, earns it . . . he who doesn't . . . pays it." You can apply the same compounding formula to your life.

Enjoy your years of exploration, knowing that when you reach your Builder phase, you will be able to make up for all the "lost time" society would have you believe you wasted in your precious youth.

If you were given 18 years to achieve something significant, what could you do? The obvious answer is—anything you want! With that much time on your hands you can achieve any objective you set for yourself. Limiting your active building period to 18 years forces you to develop a sense of urgency that will compel you to work toward your goals every day. Instead of cruising aimlessly, you'll drive a speedboat that catapults you to your destiny.

Certain people might assume the advice to explore your options for 18 years is a get-out-of-jail-free card from working, but you'll still have to support yourself. The irony is that you'll need to seriously commit to your explorations even if it seems like you're wasting your time on things that might not pan out. Even if your exploring looks outlandish, like a five-year surfing trip around the South Pacific, Hawaii, Indonesia, and Australia. The people you meet and the cultures you experience could transform your life; making that trip might be the best decision of your life. You'll never know until you do it.

Inside Megiddo Prison

When I began my own Explorer phase, I learned for myself that life would present me with unforeseen challenges. Israel has a mandatory army service of three years for males and two years for females. Serving in the Israel Defense Forces is embedded in the culture and is considered an essential rite of passage for Israeli teenagers: a duty that is shared by all, a necessary stepping-stone into civilian life.

All that is to say that I began my Explorer years doing something I didn't choose for myself, and two months after I joined the army, just as I turned 18, I found myself in a military prison. Not an ideal place to play the rebel, and not the best way to start my period of exploration, but that is how it unfolded for me.

Before I was drafted, I'd made up my mind that the only thing that I wanted to do in the army was to be a paramedic. It was my dream. Looking back, I'm not sure why I was so stubborn about it, but I was taken with the idea of being part of the medical profession, wearing a medic pin on my army shirt, saving lives and alleviating suffering. After eight weeks of basic training, my fellow new recruits and I arrived at a central army base, where we were given our assignments for the next three years. We were told to write down three preferences in order of importance. I listed paramedic as my first, second, and third options, and stated my strong desire to become a paramedic in a personal interview as well. I was certain the army would recognize my potential and strong motivation! In hindsight, I was woefully unprepared for military life.

It might seem obvious, but when you are a civilian and you want to learn something—to become someone—all options are open for you. You can undertake any course of study you'd like. The army, however, like any large, complex organization, does things differently. One doesn't simply walk in and demand a position and expect smooth sailing. The recruitment officer decides who goes where based on myriad facts including the available positions, the demand for these positions, your educational background, how well you did on your aptitude test, your physical condition—the list goes on and on.

After several days of waiting around, the recruits were called to a dusty lot at the front of the base, where buses were waiting to take us to our units.

A loudspeaker crackled and in rapid succession the new recruits were ordered to board the buses. I was called in the first group.

"Danon, Bus 31."

I looked over at Bus 31. A faded piece of cardboard in the window read "Signal Corps." I approached the officer and asked about my assignment. He looked at his papers and informed me that I was scheduled to become a multichannel high-frequency radio systems operator.

"A multi what?" I asked, dumbfounded.

He waved his hand toward the bus, instructing me to get my gear and board it immediately. I stood there, unable to move. Everyone was looking at me. I reminded myself that this was my moment of truth. If I got on that bus, I would never become a paramedic. I shook my head slowly. The officer shot me a stern look and repeated his order. I did not move.

Everyone was watching with rapt attention, wondering what would happen next. The officer was suddenly joined by a drill sergeant, a short, chubby man with a thick mustache and a malicious look in his eyes. The sergeant got in my face and shouted, "Get your butt on Bus 31, now!"

"There is a mistake. Can you please check the papers again? I am supposed to go to the paramedic course," I said in an unsteady voice.

The Explorer

He screamed in my face. "Last warning! Get on this bus now or face a military court for refusing a direct order!"

I did not move. The sergeant, tired of my antics and aware that everyone was watching us, grabbed my hand and started walking toward the bus. When we were almost there, I pulled back my hand, resisting his grip—a mistake that would cost me dearly. Exasperated, he let go of me and told me I was under arrest.

I stayed one night in a makeshift prison in the assessment center. Morning came. I heard loud shouts in the yard as the soldiers started a few drills. I was brought into a small windowless office and instructed to remain standing. The recruiting officer and the sergeant were on a bench across the room. The recruiting officer did not look at me, but the sergeant had a smirk on his face, as if he knew what was about to happen. The judge was a senior officer, a lieutenant colonel. He made a big show of looking at the papers in front of him, moving them from side to side, then asked the officer to report what happened.

After the officer gave a dry summary of my insubordination, the sergeant gave his lively version, in which I was portrayed as a destabilizing element whose insubordination could have led other soldiers to take matters into their own hands. He portrayed me as a grizzled veteran who knew what he was doing, rather than the clueless fresh-faced recruit that I was. The sergeant described in graphic detail our little confrontation, making me look like an unpredictable and violent soldier. I had to give it to him; this guy knew how to tell a story.

The judge listened with a bored expression. He waved his hand lazily toward the sergeant, ordering him to sit down, then asked for my version of what happened. In an excited tone and with animated hand movements, I shared my aspirations of becoming a medic, helping in dire situations, performing my duty in a noble way. His bored expression did not change. When I was done, he looked at me and asked, "Why did you refuse direct orders from the officer and the sergeant?"

"Because my assignment to the signal corps is a mistake?" I answered hesitantly.

"The army doesn't make mistakes," he said. "This was your assignment."

"And the paramedic course?" I blurted out, feeling like I was rapidly losing ground.

"There are no open spots. This is a prestigious course and we have too many applicants." He seemed tired of this exchange. He leaned forward in his chair and asked me, "Why did you assault the sergeant?"

I said I was just trying to break free from his grip. The judge told me my sentence would be announced in an hour. He nodded to another soldier, who escorted me back to my holding cell.

As promised, I was brought back in an hour to hear my sentence. This time the officer and the sergeant were not there. The lieutenant colonel made another show of moving papers around. He coughed a few times, then without looking directly at me, read the sentence:

"The soldier's actions were in direct violation of military codes. Not only did he refuse a direct order from a commanding officer, but when a sergeant tried to gently lead him to the bus, he attacked him. I hereby sentence the soldier to twenty-eight days in a military prison."

The Explorer

I could not believe it: twenty-eight days in a military prison? What would my parents and friends think? How would I survive a month in prison?

The officer waved his hand, and a young soldier took me back to my holding cell. This was not how I'd imagined starting my glorious service. A military prison term is something one carries with them for the rest of their service; it affects future promotions and overall advancement in the army. The next morning, I was transferred to prison.

The van that transported me and three other soldiers had one small, slimy window, but the mood inside was surprisingly cheerful. We cracked jokes, trying to look tougher than we felt, but that came to a screeching halt at the prison's main gate. When we stepped off the van, we were in a large yard in the middle of an imposing gray structure surrounded by a tall fence. We had arrived at the infamous Megiddo Prison—which also houses hardened criminals.

Although the wing dedicated to the military prison was isolated from the rest of the prisoners, the "real" prisoners were a menacing presence on the other side of the fence. Strangely enough, my father's tough love regime prepared me well for prison. I had no problem waking up early, performing meaningless, repetitive tasks, or taking cold showers. But it wasn't a fun experience, make no mistake about it. It was a grim, dirty, and depressing place, designed to make life miserable.

Somehow the twenty-eight days passed, and I was sent back to the assessment center. In the same small office where I heard my shocking sentence, I encountered the same bored officer at his desk piled with papers. He nodded at me, as if surprised to see I was out so soon, and asked arrogantly, "Have you learned your lesson?"

"I believe so, sir," I said cautiously, not sure where the conversation was going.

"Good," he said. "I am sending you to become a . . ." He shuffled some papers until he found a thin file with my name written in purple ink at the top. He opened the file and took out a single sheet of paper. I swallowed hard.

He squinted his eyes and said, "A multichannel high-frequency radio systems operator."

I could not believe it. Was he pulling my leg?

"No, it can't be," I blurted in utter confusion. "I served my sentence. Can I please start my medical training?"

He snickered. "The army is not here to accommodate your wishes. Report to the signal corps base by tomorrow morning."

I looked at him in disbelief, trying to shake this nightmare of a scenario. I tried to say something, but words didn't come out. He gave me a stern look and said, "If you are not going to report to the signal corps base, this will be your second instance of insubordination. You'll leave me no choice but to send you back to prison."

He waited a moment, and when he realized that I wasn't going to respond, his tone softened a bit. He coughed and said, "Think carefully about what you are going to say next. Are you going to report to the signal corps tomorrow morning?"

I shook my head no.

Now he seemed to be at a loss for words.

This time I was sentenced to fourteen days in Megiddo. Back in the van with the tiny, dirty window, I considered the fact that I wasn't managing things very well so far. My predicament was ridiculously bad. Only three months in the army, and already twice in military prison.

With a heavy heart, I entered the prison again. Nothing had changed—the same dreadful routine, same horrendous food, same poor living conditions. But during my extra time for reflection, I came to understand that I can adapt to whatever life throws at me. I didn't have any epiphanies, but I learned something important about myself: I will go to great lengths to get what I want. I will go through hell and fire to get it. This knowledge came in handy three years later when I made the difficult decision to leave my family and friends in pursuit of another life in the United States.

After my fourteen days were up, I was sent back to the assessment center. I was relieved to find out that my old nemesis was not there. This time another officer reviewed my file. He asked me to sit down, which I took as a good omen. He made a number of notes on my file, removed his glasses, gave me a puzzled look, and asked, "Are you looking to be dishonorably discharged?"

This question caught me by surprise, even though it probably shouldn't have. Many of the soldiers in military prison had talked about how to get released from the army and start whatever life was waiting for them outside, but I wasn't one of them. It was my duty to serve, even if it was shockingly clear to me that I didn't fit the profile of an ideal soldier.

"No, sir. I want to complete my military service as a paramedic."

As I uttered those words, I wondered how many more times I would have to say them. Is this what my entire military service would come to? An endless repetition of the same act?

The saga started to take on a surreal quality. I braced myself for my "new" assignment as a multichannel high-frequency radio systems operator, but the officer did not instruct me to report to the signal corps. Instead, he gave me an inquisitive look.

"What is this obsession you have with becoming a paramedic? You know it's a prestigious position, and we usually don't send someone with your background to such a course."

With my background? I had turned from a promising teenager to what—a hardened ex-con?

I took a deep breath.

"I have paid a heavy price for my mistakes, sir. I am only three months into my service, and I want to stay in the army. I deserve a second chance, and you will see, if you send me to this course, I will end up with the highest marks." I looked him in the eyes and added in a serious tone, "This is my promise to you."

He frowned and said, "You don't need to promise me anything." He gave me another searching look, nodding his head sagely as if considering the merits of my appeal. I was asked to wait outside the office for an answer. An hour later, an alarmingly thin soldier approached with an envelope in his hand. He handed it to me wordlessly and left. I took a deep breath and opened the envelope. Inside was a formal letter instructing me to show up for the next paramedic course two weeks later. In the bottom left corner, the officer had written in red marker, "Good luck."

It was time to go home. I'd sent my parents a postcard from Megiddo, saying that I was in training and would not be able to communicate with them for some time. My fellow soldiers told me it would be postmarked from an anonymous base, but when I got home, my mother hugged me tightly. My postcard had arrived with the stamp of Megiddo Prison. To my surprise, my father was visibly proud of me. He patted me on the shoulder and told me that "a real soldier needs to spend time in a military prison. It shows you have character." It was one of the few compliments I ever received from my father.

I finished the paramedic course with the highest marks in the cohort. But what had I learned?

First, that messing with large and imposing institutions has real consequences. Second, that I have a bit of steel in me. If I want to do something, I'm willing to pay a serious price for it. In hindsight, that was not the best way to learn those lessons, but it's the path I took. I hope this book saves you from learning lessons like these the hard way.

Military service also forced me to learn how to deal with different kinds of people under stressful circumstances. In the army, you interact with soldiers from diverse backgrounds in a pressure-cooker type situation. This is a significant challenge with tangible benefits, and it's one I encourage you to undertake. You don't have to join the army, but you should spend time in a place where you must get along with many people who are not exactly like you.

The growth takes place when you are forced to try to understand how other people think and why they behave the way they do. Social friction compels you to face your own weaknesses as much as the irritating traits of others. You might not want to, but you must if you're going to have a good relationship with any diverse group of people.

Don't underestimate the soft skills of getting along with diverse types of people, being able to understand and relate to them, and putting aside your own preferences. People want to be around people who make them feel comfortable, who are easy to be around, who understand that their own needs are not the only factor in a relationship. If people like you, you will go far.

Minimize Your Regrets

One of the key benefits of allowing yourself to explore your options for 18 years is that it will minimize your regrets—and the fewer regrets, the better, since you never know what life may throw at you. If you wait around for something important to happen to you, you may never get to do it.

When I worked for the Intercontinental Hotels Group in London, I befriended a regional director who was well versed in the politics of this massive organization. I was in my late twenties and George was in his early fifties, and he became one of my Mentors. After a while, he told me his big dream: to travel to the southern tip of Argentina to explore Patagonia, a wild and remote region with majestic glaciers and imposing mountains.

George had maps of Patagonia pinned to his office walls. Whenever we had tea together, he shared with me, for what felt like the thousandth time, how he would get to Patagonia, where he would stay, and the best hiking routes to a famous glacier called Perito Moreno. That was usually where I stopped him and asked when he was planning to go. He would look at me and say, "You do realize, don't you, that if I am going to go away for a couple of weeks, my job might not wait for me?"

The Explorer

Years later, a colleague told me that George retired from the company at sixty-five and promptly boarded a plane to Argentina. On the first mountain he climbed, he suffered a massive heart attack and died at once. My ever-optimistic wife, upon hearing this sad story, said, "At least he died fulfilling his dream."

That's one way to look at it, but I don't think that's what George had in mind when he embarked on his long-wished-for adventure. George's story is an extreme example of what could happen if you wait too long to act on your dreams: They can slip away from you in the most mysterious way.

If you have a compelling dream, go ahead and pursue it *right now*. I know it sounds simple enough, but I have seen repeatedly with my coaching clients that most people are comfortable delaying big decisions like this. You don't want to have major regrets later in life. You want to be able to tell yourself you gave it all you got over the years. If at the end of the day you find out that you're simply not cut out for it, at least you'll know what *not* to dedicate your life to.

We like to believe there's time for everything, that we can do whatever we want at any point in our lives, but that's a cruel illusion. Timing is incredibly important. Start minimizing your regrets in the Dreamer phase and keep doing so throughout your entire life. Talk to Givers and ask them what they would have done differently. Odds are, you'll hear a lot of woulda, coulda, shouldas. They'll talk about things they wish they had done, specific actions they should have taken. You don't want to feel like that when you reach their age.

You want to explore your dreams like Chris Pariso did. Growing up in New Hampshire, Chris dreamed about one thing: becoming a pastry chef. When he graduated from the prestigious Le Cordon Bleu Culinary School, he fulfilled that dream—then worked in the industry for five years only to find that his heart was not in it. As he put it, "It's really hard to have a meaningful relationship when you're working seventy hours a week and you're exhausted when you come home."

It's not easy to decide to walk away from something after you've invested so much in it, but that's exactly what you need to do while you're still young and can rebound and move on. Chris realized at one point that he wanted to do more with his life than bake. He went back to school, this time leveraging his love of math, and eventually became a data analyst—but it almost doesn't matter what he became. The lesson is in what he had to go through to realize that his first dream was not right for him. It was a painful realization, but he approached it the right way: by doing everything he could to fulfill it. He enrolled at a top culinary school and graduated from the program, then worked for five years in the industry. Five years is a good chunk of time to find out whether you're on the right path. It's long enough to see you through the first awkward steps toward applying what you've learned to real life, which is often vastly different.

Let's say you learn in culinary school that bread dough must rest for a full night in the fridge before you can bake it, but when you start working in a restaurant, the chef tells you to put the dough in the fridge for two hours and then start baking immediately. There's an enormous difference between theory and practice.

When Chris looks back at his life, I guarantee you he won't be saying to himself, "I should have tried harder to succeed at being a pastry chef. I should have gone to a better school, then worked for a few more years at it . . ." By eliminating all the "coulda, woulda, shouldas," Chris made sure he wouldn't look back with regret on this exploration. He can cross this dream off his list forever—and that is the proper way to think about fulfilling your dreams. You want to give each dream your utmost consideration, effort, and energy, using all the resources you have. If you still come up short, you'll know you gave it your all and you'll have no regrets about it. As John Barrymore said, "A man is not old until regrets take the place of dreams."

You need to do things at the right time and at the right place. Sounds simple, doesn't it? When I backpacked around the world in my twenties, I decided to try parachuting from an airplane in New Zealand. It was an awesome experience, exciting and exhilarating. Recently, my daughter Maya convinced me to do it again. Sitting high above the clouds, my feet dangling in the air as I was next in line to jump, I realized too late that it was not one of my best decisions. My outlook had changed drastically over the past twenty-five years; this time I was all too aware of the finality of it all if the parachute didn't open. When I jumped into the open sky, the happy and carefree feeling I had the first time was replaced by cold, hard fear and a nausea that lingered after the parachute opened safely. Certain things must happen at a certain time. Trying to do them too early in life, or too late, might produce an effect opposite to what you desire.

Although I try to minimize my regrets, I know I can't eliminate them completely. My biggest fear is that life will just go by—day after day, week after week, month after month, year after year. If I had no big dreams to pursue, my life would be spent, like a deep well that's gone dry over the years. There is no such thing as a life with no regrets; that would go against human nature. We are wired to constantly consider what could have been and where we could have done better. But minimizing regrets puts us in a wonderful place.

If you really want to do something, and if it doesn't hurt the people you love, nine times out of ten, you should go for it. Make it happen. You never know if you'll get another chance. Life is fleeting. Act on the important things on a consistent basis. You will never have zero regrets but living with only a few is an acceptable trade-off.

Macho's Cholesterol-Free Eggs

To get in the zone where you are truly pursuing a dream to the fullest, you'll have to summon your full attention. The ability to focus on one thing over an extended time is what leads to success. Multitasking just doesn't work! Researchers from Stanford University asked eighty young adults to do two things at the same time, such as texting while watching TV, and the results were overwhelming: the students could not recall what happened on TV, even though they'd just seen it. Too many people habitually multitask with their life choices, simultaneously pursuing several avenues to try to determine what they're good at. What you need is the full-on determination of someone who deliberately burns bridges to find out if one they're on leads to the promised land.

On my last surfing trip to Costa Rica, I met Macho, a young guy in his late twenties who rented out ATVs. He greeted me warmly when I came into his shop, as if I were a long-lost friend. Macho was heavily muscled, sported a deep tan, and had an intense stare. He told me that in addition to renting ATVs, he organized day tours to the rainforest and to a secret waterfall; I signed up. I got to talk to Macho several times on the tour, which also involved visited his poultry farm, where he triumphantly announced that his hens laid eggs with the lowest cholesterol levels in Costa Rica. He had another business as a property manager for wealthy Americans with beach houses, and to top it off, he was trying to start a surf safari company.

We sat in the shade of a massive tree at his chicken farm, engulfed in dry white dust. Macho said, "Man, I am tired. I am running ragged. From five A.M. to eight P.M. every day, trying to manage all my businesses."

I said, "Your lifestyle is more fitting for a trader on Wall Street, not someone who lives on a stretch of paradise right next to the Pacific Ocean."

He chuckled humorlessly and said nothing.

"Let me get it straight," I said. "You're running four different businesses. The ATV company, the egg business, the property management business, and the surf safari outfit."

"That's right," he said proudly. "And each one could be huge"—he spread his hands and gestured toward the chickens— "if I'm serious about it. With my special feeding formula, I could become the largest supplier of low-cholesterol eggs in this region."

"And the other businesses?"

"All huge potential," Macho claimed. "I could be the largest property manager in the area, the biggest tour operator, and the biggest surf safari company."

"But you can't be all of those at the same time," I said.

He shot me a quick, puzzled look, shaking his head like a teacher who is disappointed by a slow student. "If I continue to work like this for the next five years, I can make it happen for all these businesses."

"Have you considered doubling down on the most promising business—let's say the egg business for one year—and then assessing the results?"

"You don't understand," said Macho, pronouncing each word slowly as if explaining something complicated to a child. "*All* my businesses have huge potential."

I wished Macho the best of luck. Who knows, maybe he is one of those rare individuals who can achieve phenomenal success in several areas, but they're few and far between. You have much better chances on realizing your dreams if you double down on them one at a time.

Let's Talk About Money

There is no need to try to make serious money before you turn 36. In fact, there are significant drawbacks to striving to build a solid foundation while still exploring. Your freedom to explore is much more important than trying to meet any self-imposed financial goals at this early stage of your life. It's true that money is the traditional measure of success in a capitalist economy, but I have never thought net worth should determine personal worth. Breathe easy, my friend. You have more time than you'll ever need to build your financial foundation. You don't have to do it in your twenties.

Before the age of 36, I had no money. No savings, no retirement plan, and quite honestly, no worries. The year I turned 36, I became vice president of marketing for a publicly traded

The Explorer

technology company. My salary hit six figures for the first time and continued to rise year after year. It all happened at the right time.

I know that runs counter to what you've heard—that you must start saving from the age of four and focus on making money as soon as you're on your own. Sure, if you can start saving money at an early age, go ahead and do it. The financial logic is sound. But focusing only on money at the expense of pursuing your dreams will have a more negative impact on your life than your savings rate.

Obviously, you need to support yourself, and if you have a family, your loved ones. But don't let yourself become obsessed with dollars and cents. Become obsessed with fulfilling the potential of your dreams. The money will flow in during your Builder years, from 36 to 54.

Advances in the medical field mean that most of today's Dreamers will live to one hundred. If you have one hundred years on this Earth, you have enough time to make serious money after you turn 36. Your twenties and thirties are the time to prepare, explore, and find out where you can be a world champion.

Young people the world over are already doing this. They're getting married older, waiting to start families, minimizing their expenses, avoiding houses they can't afford. They get it: This is the time for exploration, and no one will persuade them that the old ways are right for them. They know they have time to seriously explore their options and prepare for the next stage.

There's a good chance no one has ever asked you what you really want to do with your life. If they did, you were probably way too young to know, and whatever you came up with sounded good, so you went for it. Doesn't it make sense to take your time to find out what you are good at? To figure out what you love to do and what are your natural gifts? There's no need to worry about how you measure up if you're earnestly pursuing your dream and giving it all you can.

Because I enjoyed staying in hotels, when I went to college, I chose to major in hospitality management. Not a highly scientific way of going about a major life decision, but that's youth for you! It was the equivalent of deciding to learn Japanese after falling in love with sushi. Like most young people, I felt pressured to choose a major: to do *something* and do it *now*.

The 18 years of the Explorer phase are your time to find your life's true calling. You have time to fully commit to each dream, without shortcuts. An old Portuguese proverb teaches us, "Think of many things; do one." The ability to dedicate yourself to one dream at a time without entertaining ideas of plans B or C or D is a hallmark of the serious Explorer.

The only way to find out whether you're on the right path is to walk it every day for several years. You'll need to summon your courage to follow your own path. It will get dicey at times and setbacks will test your perseverance, but it's in challenging times that we discover how far we're willing to go.

The Journey Ahead

So here you are, an intrepid Explorer, on your exciting journey of self-discovery! You'll dedicate the ages of 18 to 36 to finding out exactly what you want to do and creating a solid plan for achieving it. As you set out to explore your dreams, you may feel pressure from yourself and others to "act your age" and

The Explorer

be responsible—whatever that means. But being an Explorer is vastly different from being irresponsible. It assumes a great deal of responsibility for ensuring that your personal and professional life will be full and rewarding. It can be challenging to walk to the beat of a different drum, but if you do what's expected of you rather than what you expect of yourself, you may please others and leave yourself unsatisfied.

As an Explorer, you answer only to *your* dreams, even if the world—including your family and friends—expects something completely different. You may feel pressure to take a particular job or stick with the one you have, even if it's lousy. You may have taken on too many financial obligations too soon and become risk averse at the point in your life when taking risks is the most important thing you can do.

If you've already assumed a mortgage (or two), maxed out your credit cards, taken long-term loans, or incurred other debts—stop right there. Do not take on more debt or obligations. Start paying it off now. Your freedom to explore is at stake here.

If all you want at this point is to make lots of money, you might make it happen. But then what happens when you're rich? What exactly are you going to do? Even if you're one of the lucky ones who can retire early, you could very easily get bored and lose your sense of purpose. Most people in their twenties mean well but are ill-prepared to realize their dreams. They are full of ambition but lack the skills, knowledge, and confidence to realize their potential. It's not as simple as making up your mind about the best way forward. You could be bound by your own sense of honor, by the expectations others place on you, or by your inability to say no. What you need is a push, and that usually comes at the most unexpected time.

A Gentle Push

When I completed my army service, I was twenty-one years old. My dream was to move to the United States and start a new life, but I made little practical progress. I spent most of my time with my girlfriend, who had no desire to leave Israel and was planning our future there together. Her vision included me working in her uncle's car dealership on the outskirts of Tel Aviv. In her mind, we would have a grand time doing this—and when you're that young and the world around you seems daunting and uncertain, sometimes any opportunity seems like a good one. I was torn between my dream of independence and the prospect of a supposedly safe path as a used car salesperson.

Into this dilemma stepped my rebel uncle. He was someone who always did the unexpected, who lived life on his own terms. He rode a motorcycle, had a cool leather jacket, and said exactly what he wanted to say, with no thought to the consequences. At one point he left his family and lived in a cave on the beach. My mother told him about the situation with my girlfriend and my dream of starting fresh in the United States, and one day, out of the blue, he came to my house and took me for a spin. After an exhilarating motorcycle ride, we stopped in a park next to a small lake where kids were casting lines from makeshift fishing rods. We sat on the grass and watched the sun flicker on the still water. A warm wind blew gently around us, and birds chirped in the tree above us.

He turned to me and said, "You know, you can make something big with your life."

I smiled and nodded, not sure what he meant.

He turned his gaze to the lake for a few minutes before addressing me again. This time he didn't look at me directly. He said quietly, almost to himself, "But first you need to pass a test."

"What kind of a test?" I asked, puzzled.

In a no-nonsense tone he said, "You need to move to the US and prove that you've got what it takes to make it there, starting from scratch."

"Why can't I stay in Israel and try my luck here?" I asked, thinking about the car dealership. All of a sudden, working there didn't seem like such a bad idea.

He shook his head and said, "Your destiny is not here." He gestured at the lake, then cupped his hands to show how small the lake was. He looked me in the eye to make sure I understood his point. When he was satisfied, he opened his arms wide and said, "Find an ocean and see if you can thrive there."

I took a couple of deep breaths.

He patted my shoulder and said gently, "Don't mess it up."

The following weeks were tough as I wrestled with the decision through many sleepless nights. Then one morning I woke up and knew it was time. I shared the news with my parents. My mother cried quietly while my father embraced me tightly and said, "I will miss you." It was much more difficult than I'd imagined. I waited another week before talking to my girlfriend.

Even though I'd rehearsed the conversation in my mind several times, when it came down to it, I didn't say what I wanted to say. She cried inconsolably and the whole experience was miserable for both of us.

But I had made up my mind. I knew what I had to do.

Two weeks later I boarded a plane from Tel Aviv to Miami with a one-way ticket. My family came to the airport to see me off, and my girlfriend unexpectedly showed up as well. It was an emotional departure. When the plane took off, I realized that I'd paid a heavy price to embark on this journey. I wondered if it would be worth it.

I know now that it was.

Sometimes all we need is someone who will look us in the eye, confirm what we need to do, and give us permission to move forward. If we respond, we can change the arc of our lives, but responding isn't easy when you're young and full of yourself. If you think the world owes you something, you're going to miss your chance to get ahead.

The Weed Garden

In my twenties I often felt like I knew better than anyone else. I didn't really listen; I just nodded and smiled. I wonder how many opportunities I missed because I didn't take things seriously.

Back when I was a penniless student at Daytona Beach Community College, a friend and I decided to try our hand at gardening. We bought a beat-up van that rattled and hissed like it was on its deathbed, an ancient lawn mower, a shovel, a rusty garden rake, a folding hand saw, and three pairs of large pruning scissors. We eked out a living in the first couple months, but it wasn't what we'd dreamed about. We knew that to get to the big league, the stately mansions where the rich

The Explorer

people lived, we needed a lucky break: someone who would take a chance on our fledgling business.

I don't remember exactly how we did it, but we landed a prime assignment at one of the large houses next to the Halifax River. The owner walked us through his magnificent property, with swaying palm trees, beautiful red flowers, and exposed tree roots that snaked around the property. At the entrance to the house was a large area that was covered with thick, tall weeds that looked out of place. The owner saw us looking at it and turned to us with a broad smile. "I love this untamed area," he said. "Whatever you do, don't touch it. It looks wild, but this is exactly how I want it: a piece of wild nature right at the front door."

We nodded and moved on. There was plenty of work, that was for sure. We started right away. We were young, fit, and motivated, and after a week of hard labor, the place was transformed. We felt like we'd restored the massive garden to its former glory. All was in order except the wild area near the house. It seemed out of place, like a coffee stain on a white linen suit. We thought back for a minute about what the owner told us not to do, then looked at each other and nodded in silent agreement. Over the next hour we took care of this outcrop of weeds, flattening it completely. Then we felt like our work was finally done. We waited in the shade of a large palm at the front of the garden for the owner to come appraise our excellent work.

I turned to my friend and asked, "How many references do you think we can get out of this guy?"

He considered this carefully. "We should get ten to fifteen direct references."

I was impressed. This was way more optimistic than my estimate. We sat enjoying the shade, running the numbers, getting richer by the minute. My friend peeled an orange and gave me a slice. He said, "We would need more workers. Better tools. More advertising."

I bit into the orange, thinking that this was the beginning of a promising enterprise. "You know something, we should expand beyond Daytona Beach. Once we take over this market, I suggest looking at New Smyrna Beach as our next target."

My friend beamed like this was the smartest thing in the world. "Pretty soon we can each *buy* a house like this!" he said. "We are making it!" We both laughed, feeling like we'd just won a million dollars. It was the best feeling in the world. We worked hard and created our own opportunities, and nothing could beat that.

We heard the gravel crunch under the wheels of a Jaguar as the owner arrived. His hair was slicked back, and he wore expensive sunglasses. He got out of the car and shook our hands. We walked him through the property and could see that he was pleased—but when we came in sight of the entrance, he was stricken with disbelief.

"What have you done? What have you done?" he cried in despair.

We were dumbstruck.

"Didn't I specifically say that this area was not to be touched? Why on Earth would you do something like that?"

My friend muttered something about the overall look and feel of the property, and how this area was out of touch with the rest of the landscaping. The owner stopped him, reached into his pocket for our check, and said, "I don't ever want to see you guys again. In fact, if I see your junk of a van in this town, I will personally seek out your clients and let them know how unprofessional you are."

He went into his house, and that was end of our landscaping business.

Our arrogance and stupidity did us in. We didn't listen; we thought we were smarter than our client. Worse than that, we thought we knew what was best for him. I learned a lot about humility that day, but I also learned a valuable lesson about myself: I am not suited for a career that depends on simply following directions.

Discovery of the Lost City

Hiram Bingham was an American archeologist who was fascinated by the idea of finding the lost Incan city of Machu Picchu. For hundreds of years explorers had searched for this mythical city, said to be situated on a remote Peruvian mountaintop surrounded by lush jungle.

Bingham spent years exploring South America and had exhausted his life savings on ridiculously expensive expeditions. In 1911 the Peruvian government built a new road through the jungle to move cocoa and rubber over deep river gorges, and Bingham realized it was his last chance. He was 36 at the time and had already dedicated years to exploring his dream; he could have given up and gone back to his comfortable life as a Yale lecturer. Instead, he decided to embark on one last journey and be one of the first people in the world to travel the new road.

He soon got completely lost in the jungle, and unexpectedly arrived at a farm a thousand feet above a plunging river.

The indigenous residents were shocked to see him. With a ten-year-old boy interpreting, Bingham asked about the lost city. The natives pointed up. He kept climbing. Suddenly, he came upon what he later described as "a magnificent flight of stone terraces, rising thousands of feet up the mountainside." He climbed for an hour more until he found himself in a deep forest, where he came upon a temple made of granite blocks cut with amazing precision. "Surprise followed surprise in bewildering succession," he wrote. "I climbed a marvelous stairway of granite blocks and came to a clearing in which were two of the finest structures I had ever seen. I was spellbound." Finally, after years of exploration, in his 36th year, Bingham had discovered the lost city of the Incas on an inaccessible mountaintop two thousand feet above a roaring river in the Peruvian Andes.

The joy of discovery was overwhelming. "I know of no place in the world which can compare with it. Not only has it great snow peaks looming above the clouds more than two miles overhead, gigantic precipices of many-colored granite rising sheer for thousands of feet above the foaming, roaring rapids; it has also, in striking contrast, orchids and tree ferns, the beauty of luxurious vegetation, and the mysterious witchery of the jungle."

Bingham's book, *Lost City of the Incas*, was published in 1948 and became a bestseller. He has been cited as the person upon whom the intrepid character of Indiana Jones was based. Machu Picchu is now considered one of the most important archeological discoveries in the world. When I went to Machu Picchu with my family, I stood on top of the mountain and looked down at the ruins, imagining Hiram Bingham walking there for the first time, his eyes wide at the majestic sight.

To be an Explorer, you must be willing to leave behind all that is comfortable and familiar. You must chart unfamiliar territory, knowing that the payoff could be huge—if you stick to your dream no matter what happens around you.

Follow Your Own Path

It's not easy to stay the course when you see your friends moving up in the world, buying this car or that espresso machine, putting a down payment on a starter home. But patience and belief in *your* way are required from you at this stage. Your time will come, and it will be a glorious one indeed.

If you take the time to find out exactly what you want to do—and what you are especially good at—you will have a distinct advantage over most people your age. Our society idolizes early success at the expense of more natural development; conventional wisdom would tell you not to move from job to job for fear of appearing unserious or unsettled. But the Principle of 18 will not lead to a conventional life, so why keep listening to conventional wisdom? What you need is more time to reflect, to learn about yourself and your unique gifts.

Granted, sometimes we discover what we're searching for right out of the gate. You might find your life's true calling on the first try—some people are lucky that way.

Maria, a lighthearted young woman in her mid-twenties, is one such example. She worked as a hairdresser at the Supercuts in my neighborhood in northern New Jersey. I don't have much hair left, but I went in for a trim just to share her liveliness and contagious laughter. She was a pleasure to be around, and nothing filled her with more energy and excitement than her work. She enjoyed meeting and talking to all her customers and was quite talented with the scissors (or in my case, the electric shaver).

During one of my visits, she asked me what I did for a living. I told her about the Principle of 18 and that I was planning to write this book to help people find meaning at all stages of their life. She looked at me and smiled.

"This is exactly the plan I've been following all my life," she said. "Fortunately for me, all I had was one dream, and since cutting hair is what I love to do, I plan on sticking with it!" If you're like Maria, you'll strike gold.

At the opposite end of the spectrum are those who search constantly for new experiences, become dissatisfied quickly, and move rapidly on to the next experience.

I met Imani when she was in her early thirties, and at that point her list of explorations would have made most people dizzy. She was an accomplished musician and songwriter as well as a member of a band, spoke fluent Italian, had lived in Rome for two years, worked as a professional hostess in one of Japan's elite social clubs, went to Ethiopia with the Peace Corps—and had started taking courses in interior design.

It soon became clear that Imani didn't stay in any one place or with one endeavor for awfully long. Her deepest fear was that she might get stuck somewhere with no options. As soon as she started to feel comfortable, she moved on. But the constant change had left her tired and confused. It took Imani a lot of moving around to realize that the grass wasn't always greener on the other side, and after a restless decade, she went

The Explorer

back to music. She'd finally understood that was where her heart and talents met.

It's not easy to find your path. I know that directionless feeling well. After college, I had what any objective observer would call a "lost decade": I backpacked in Nepal, India, Vietnam, and Thailand, then went to Australia and New Zealand. I returned to Israel penniless and stayed with my in-laws for five months until I found a job as a university lecturer, which I had always wanted to try. But after two years of teaching, I knew it was not enough for me. The academic world could wait; I wanted to keep exploring the real world. I went back into hospitality as director of training and development for the InterContinental hotel in Tel Aviv, where I could talk to guests every day and learn about their unique journeys through life.

Messy Endings

Making the right decision is usually associated with choosing what course of action to follow, where to place your bets. Rarely do we think about the best way to end things, but ending one journey and beginning another is surprisingly tricky. If we're focused on the horizon, we risk letting our guard down in critical moments. As an Explorer you'll be trying out different situations and searching for the one big thing you can create in your Builder stage, so it's important that you learn how to exit gracefully.

While studying at Daytona Beach Community College, I got a job as a Hebrew teacher at an impressive synagogue whose large windows looked out over manicured lawns and the Halifax River. I made twelve dollars an hour, which was a fortune for me.

The rabbi, my boss, was a no-nonsense, serious man. He told me that if I focused on teaching the children to read and write in Hebrew, I would be fine. Behind him was a framed photograph of a smiling, confident US Marine; the young man had the rabbi's eyes.

The classes were easy enough to teach. For some reason I started bragging to the kids that I was a great soccer player back in Israel, and that I could teach them cool tricks. A scrawny and energetic kid with a mop of red hair volunteered to bring a soccer ball to class. I had the sense to tell him to hold off on this idea and went to talk to the rabbi.

"The kids would love to play soccer outside after class," I said.

The rabbi gave me a stern look through his thick-rimmed glasses. "I don't recall that I am paying you to function as a soccer coach," he said dryly.

I said nothing.

"And besides, we don't have an insurance policy in case one of the kids gets hurt. So the answer is no, you cannot take them outside to play."

I nodded and left his office, thinking about the recommendation letter I would need when I transferred to Florida International University.

A year later, it was my last day at the synagogue. My Datsun 280 Z was packed to the brim and all I needed was my recommendation letter. I had asked the rabbi to prepare one for me, and he'd said it would be his pleasure.

The last day of class felt different. I knew it was unlikely I would ever come back to this place. I took special notice of the soft light streaming through the windows, and the big,

The Explorer

welcoming lawn peppered with palm trees that swayed gently in the wind. The redheaded kid raised his hand. When I nodded, he said, "We have a surprise for you on your last day."

I smiled. He leaned back, opened his backpack, and out came a brand-new soccer ball. All my students had signed it, thanking me for the time we spent together, wishing me luck in Miami. It was a great gift.

The ginger kid said, "What do you think about going outside for a game of soccer?"

Everyone else had left for the day; it was just me and the kids. "What could go wrong?" I thought. "We'll have couple of games, and that'll be it. A nice memory to give the kids of their cool teacher."

Five minutes later we were outside. I assigned the teams and we started playing. The sun was shining, a light breeze caressed our faces, the river was flowing nearby. It was great. Suddenly I heard a cry.

The ginger kid was lying on the grass, holding his foot, tears streaming down his face. I rushed over. He had stumbled over a root. It didn't look good; he couldn't move at all. An ambulance came twenty minutes later in a cascade of light and sound, followed by the boy's worried parents. His ankle was badly sprained.

The rabbi was summoned back to the synagogue, and after the ambulance left, he called me to his office. I walked in with a heavy heart, holding the soccer ball. When I knocked on the door, the dreary feeling intensified. The rabbi was standing by the photograph of the Marine, and for the first time, I noticed that the young man was not in any of the newer family portraits.

When I entered, the rabbi said angrily, "Do you realize what you have done?"

"I made a mistake. I am sorry," I said, embarrassed.

He shook his head as if he had given up on me.

I didn't blame him. He'd told me what not to do, and I turned around and did the exact opposite. There were no excuses. I'd messed up big, and we both knew it. If I was looking for compassion, it became clearer by the second that it wasn't going to happen.

He stared at me as if trying to penetrate my soul. I averted my eyes. He sighed, walked to his desk, and pulled out an envelope out of a drawer. He tapped the desk with it for a moment, then opened it and removed a typed letter.

"Do you know what this is?"

I had an uncomfortable feeling that I did.

The rabbi fixed his gaze on me. "You have been an outstanding teacher here for one year. The students adore you; the parents love you . . ." He chuckled without humor. "Well, up until today, that is." He read the beginning of the letter. "It is my sincere pleasure to write this letter of recommendation for Eyal Danon . . ."

He shook his head again, then tore up the letter. "You will not get a reference from this synagogue."

"But . . . what will I do in Miami?" I blurted.

He said quietly, "You might not realize this now, but I am doing you a big favor."

He didn't even shake my hand; that's how angry he was with me.

I left the office with a heavy heart and an uncertain future. The rabbi was right; I never forgot the lesson, and never will.

At the time, I thought his approach was insensitive, unbefitting of a spiritual person who believes in second chances. But he was right. My behavior brought harm to his organization. I deserved that punishment, and thinking about it now, I came off easy. It could have ended a lot worse. The rabbi was acting as a Mentor—the tough kind, for sure, but these are the lessons that stick with you.

Ending anything is complicated. It's amazingly easy to slip in the last leg. You might feel that it doesn't matter, that you've reached the end of a particular phase and you're moving on, but that's a mistake. Every step on your journey counts. Ending each meaningful experience in the best way is crucial. Make the end count as much as the beginning.

Transition Plan: From Explorer to Builder

You can start working on your plan the year you turn 33. By that time, you'll have explored your key dreams, including any new ones that came up during your exploring years, and should be on your way to solidifying what must be done in the Builder stage, from age 36 to 54. You have three years to create a master plan for the next phase of your life!

When I ask my coaching clients about their plans, the response I usually get is along the lines of "You mean for this month?" Sometimes they talk about their goals for the year, especially if we're close to the beginning of a new year. Almost never does someone cite their goals for the next few years, let alone a stretch as long as 18 years. I guarantee you that there is no resource out there that will walk you through such an extended period. When I ask my clients what they can achieve in 18 years, I usually get a look asking, "Is this a trick question?"

I get it. If we look at such an extended period, so many things can and will happen that that we can't predict. We all crave certainty, and it's a lot easier to talk about what we can accomplish this week or next month. Anything longer than that feels like a wild guess. Why bother with something so far ahead that we have no control over?

The beauty of the Principle of 18 is that it gives us a canvas big enough to paint our life stories on. With all that time on your hands and a good plan, a willing heart, and the passion to carry it forward, you can achieve anything you want. Even your biggest, most daring dreams can be realized in the Builder phase when you break down complex undertakings into manageable steps.

As Antoine de Saint-Exupéry, author of *The Little Prince*, said, "A goal without a plan is just a wish." One practical way to create your Builder plan is to identify separate categories and list what you want to achieve in each one. Here are seven categories you might work with:

1) Your family/relationships
4) Your skills/expertise
5) Your career/business/sources of income
6) Your physical/mental health
7) Your emotions/feelings
8) Your sources of joy
9) Your spirituality/inspiration

Go back and review your notes every month. Revise them until you have a beautifully thought-out plan for building each category of your empire. Then break down each category even further.

The Explorer

Let's take the category of career and money. You should work on the next level of detail here by having five sections in your Explorer notebook:

- **Goals:** Which outcomes are you are looking to achieve after 18 years?
- **Resources:** What do you need to get started? This could be anything from financial literacy to people who can help you on your journey.
- **Steps:** This is the nitty-gritty process of getting it done. Like you did in the Dreamer phase, develop every step, even if there are forty or fifty of them. You will have time to walk the entire length of your journey as a Builder.
- **Challenges/Obstacles:** Identify potential roadblocks and think about how you would overcome them. The more prepared you are, the smoother your path will be.
- **Mindset:** How will you motivate yourself?

Knowing that your Builder phase is finite, why not give it your all? Focus on what you're passionate about now, rather than thinking you'll get to it later. Instead of working forty long years at 50% commitment, you can work for 18 years at 100% and make every day count. As a Builder, you'll have the precious opportunity to create your own empire. You will have enough time to get where you're going if you are focused, dedicated, and energized. These 18 years arrive at exactly the time when your energy and passion are at their peak. As a Builder, you should devour the world as you scale your own mountain!

Key Ideas for Explorers

Exhaust each dream before you move on to the next. It's not enough to give a halfhearted effort and then decide, "This is not for me." Fully exhaust the potential of each one of your dreams, even if it takes several years.

Take risks. This is the best time to take major risks. A risk-taking attitude will serve you well in the Builder phase, too, but the stakes will be higher then. As an Explorer, you don't have a lot to lose. Start taking more risks so you learn how to push beyond your comfort zone.

Don't obsess over money. It's more important to find your passion and plan for your Builder years. Be smart about spending and don't make major financial commitments.

Start planning for your Builder stage when you're 33. Take these three years to develop a comprehensive plan for achieving your goals.

Handle each ending mindfully. It's amazingly easy to mess up at the end of a significant chapter in your life. Make sure to approach your endings with grace and consideration.

THE BUILDER
The Joy of Achievement

From 36 to 54

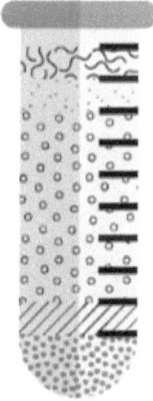

36 to 54
Builder

"What is not started today is never finished tomorrow."
—Johann Wolfgang von Goethe

NORTH STAR

The Builder years are about the joy of achievement. This is the time to get serious about your chosen profession and accomplish your goals, but it's also important to remember to enjoy the process. It's easy to get ultra-competitive when you're driving yourself hard every day but take a deep breath. You can do this without making it a grim daily slog. Be patient with the people you care about. Don't work yourself to death. Don't forget to laugh often.

This is the time to focus and double down on a single area of your professional life. What superpowers could you develop that will make you unbeatable? What unique skills and perspectives could catapult you to the top of your game? When you know, you can draft your blueprint for success. Each new experience is a brick for you to lay on your solid foundation. You'll build your castle walls brick by brick, until the day when you look down from the top of your castle, feel the cool wind in your face, and realize that you've made your dreams come true.

The key to creating something extraordinary as a Builder is to take a few big professional risks along the way, even when you're not sure how they will play out. Don't get me wrong: If you live by the Principle of 18, you'll be far ahead of most people you know. But to be extraordinary in your Builder phase you'll have to take on more risk than you're comfortable with. It can be challenging to push yourself outside of your comfort zone when you spot opportunities, but bold action and a growth mindset will serve you well. This is the time to make your mark on the world.

All you need is someone who will take a chance on you by giving you an opening through which you can wriggle. One person who looks you in the eye, sees your potential, and takes a chance on you. From there, it's up to you to expand the small opening into a breakthrough that could change the course of your life. It will be up to you to prove that person right—which is exactly what I did when the assessment officer decided to send me to the paramedic course. I did not disappoint him, but more importantly, I did not disappoint myself.

If someone wants to help you start something or get you out of trouble, you owe it to yourself to come through for them. After a while, a pattern will emerge. Influential people will start placing larger bets on you, giving you more opportunities to shine.

In your previous stage as an Explorer, you did all the experimentation necessary to discover your calling. You explored which unique gifts will help you answer it. You meticulously mapped out your route and identified the key milestones and pitfalls along the way.

The Builder

Now, as a Builder, it's finally time to get dead serious about executing your vision on a large scale. It's time to put your ambitions, hopes, and dreams to the test and find out what you're made of. This is an exciting phase! Keep in mind that you'll need to say no more often than you'd like because time is limited. You must double down on the one thing you're building and minimize everything else.

Strive to eliminate doubts like "Am I doing the right thing?" or "Should I be doing something else?" This is not the time to second-guess yourself. Learn to act with certainty, knowing that by the end of these 18 years, you will reach your destination. You've already invested years in exploring who you are and what you need to accomplish in this world. Have faith in the work you've done. You formulated a plan, and now you'll see it take shape.

Adopt the mindset that each failure is an opportunity to improve. Treat failure as a learning opportunity and go at it again with a different approach. In the words of Winston Churchill, "Success consists of going from failure to failure without loss of enthusiasm." Commit to yourself; don't give up on your dreams, no matter what. Churchill again: "Success is not final; failure is not fatal: it is the courage to continue that counts."

Act with a sense of urgency. Getting things done efficiently is different from doing busywork or dashing from one thing to the other. It is about taking care of what you know is important while minimizing distractions. Being a Builder is about showing up, doing honest work, and acting on opportunities as they arise.

Ride the Success Train

My father used to say that everyone gets at least three opportunities in life to realize their dreams, regardless of their status or position. The success train is always moving, huffing and puffing somewhere close to you; but we can only spot it, make a run for it, and jump aboard at certain points. Most people, my father would say with his finger raised for emphasis, probably 99% of them, won't be able to recognize the success train, even though it's out there right now, calling out your name, urging you to jump.

His theory was that most people are simply too busy working, making a living, paying the bills, making ends meet. They don't have the time or mindset to recognize the opportunities that present themselves. But even if you have big dreams, and opportunity knocks at your door, and you're one of the lucky few who can recognize it, only a tiny percentage of people will go for it.

I was mesmerized as a kid by the story of the success train, especially the final twist: Even though only 1% of people see the three major opportunities coming their way, most of them are too scared to drop everything and leap. That piqued my interest. Why on Earth would someone miss out on such grand and rare opportunities? If you can see the train coming and you know it could lead you to your destination, why wouldn't you jump on it?

Only after I became a Mentor did I realize that my father was right. Most of us are too scared to jump on any train—even one bound for success—if we don't know where it will take us, how long the journey will last, what it will cost, and what we'll face along the way. Even people with the gift of recognizing

The Builder

tremendous opportunities are reluctant to commit. Most people are simply not willing to abandon everything they're doing. They'll let the opportunity of a lifetime slide by rather than jump into the abyss on a leap of faith.

It's true; embarking on a new path could result in real, painful losses. Success is never guaranteed, and it's easy to be paralyzed by thoughts about defeat. Our fears often prevent us from reaching out and claiming what is ours to take.

When I was director of marketing for a midsize technology company, I decided to change how we ran our annual customer conference. Until that point, it had taken place without a lot of fanfare in windowless banquet halls in small hotels. We'd spent a lot of money on things from analysts to public relations to social media, but nothing had created a *wow* effect in our market. We were spread too thin. I decided to double down by allocating half of my annual marketing budget to this one event.

We moved the conference to San Francisco and paid the city $100,000 to cordon off the iconic Union Square for our exclusive event. When I landed the night before, the city was gloomy and foggy. It was also cooler than I'd expected, and sudden gushes of wind and rain added to the dreary picture.

My room at the Hyatt Union Square overlooked the square; I went to sleep that night hoping the weather would improve by morning. It did not. I'd put a deposit on the hotel's grand ballroom for a plan B, and I needed to decide by eleven A.M., if we are going to hold the annual conference indoors or outdoors.

The rain continued. At eleven A.M., it was a steady drizzle. I texted my director of events that I needed five more minutes to decide. The Weather Channel showed a 30% chance of rain for the evening. The *Farmer's Almanac* was no help. I was pacing back and forth in my hotel room, looking out at the gray sky and windswept square. If I took a wrong turn, there was no turning back. The hotel had made it clear they couldn't set up the ballroom for five hundred people at a moment's notice; in fact, if we didn't take it, they would rent it out to another party.

I took a deep breath and texted my director of events: "Union Square."

Miraculously, the weather improved by evening. The rain stopped and the wind eased up. The event started with dancers who formed a giant dragon, accompanied by drummers who created a hypnotic rhythm. The square was beautifully lit, we had great live music, the food and drinks were outstanding, and the evening turned out to be a massive success.

The next morning, in front of all my colleagues and hundreds of employees, the CEO promoted me to vice president of marketing. I was surprised, but not as surprised as some of my colleagues, who'd been hoping for that position for a long time. My decision to double down and take a risk had paid off in ways I hadn't even anticipated.

Play to your Strengths

The first time I competed in a martial arts tournament was not one of my life's highlights. My body was tense, my heart was racing, my mouth was dry, and I was in no condition to win any fight. I was easily eliminated in the first round. I felt defeated but stayed to watch the rest of the tournament. In walked a young man, dragging his left leg, ready to enter the sparring ring. "Poor guy," I thought, sure he would join me on

The Builder

the bench before long. I couldn't help noticing that he didn't seem nervous at all. In fact, he was smiling and waving to his friends, who happened to be sitting next to me. I turned to one of them and asked if the fighter had been injured in an accident; his friend said he was born with a deformed leg.

When the fight began, I saw that this guy had an interesting technique. He used his weak leg to block kicks, and when he had a chance, he whipped out a ferocious turning side kick with his good leg that caught his opponent in the midsection. He won the first fight fair and square and went all the way to the final match using just this one perfect kick.

He lost the finals match, but I'll never forget what I learned watching him: Even if you have only one weapon in your arsenal, you can still win. This guy focused on his core strength and was a formidable fighter by doubling down on what he did best.

Instead of working on broad skills and strengths, most people are better served by mastering a few key things that become their secret weapons. Obviously, you can have as many hobbies as you like; they usually make you a more interesting person. But one single area of expertise should consume most of your energy as a Builder.

Many people try to excel in multiple areas, citing innovators and visionaries like Leonardo da Vinci, the original "Renaissance man." Not only he was he an artistic genius, but he also studied nature, mechanics, anatomy, physics, architecture, and weaponry. Da Vinci created accurate, workable designs for a helicopter, a submarine, and a military tank, all inventions that would not come to fruition for centuries. He was, wrote

Sigmund Freud, "like a man who awoke too early in the darkness, while the others were all still asleep."

For the rest of us, it's hard enough to excel at *one* thing. Count yourself lucky if you can excel at two. As one of my Mentors told me, "If you want to be the world champion in something, you must focus on the one area where you know you can excel, and just do it over and over, until you get to a level that very few people can match." It's all about mastery through repetition.

Taking Risks

You can't expect to know everything, but if you can adapt quickly to changing situations and take appropriate risks, you will find yourself in interesting situations. If you can take a deep breath and go with the flow, you'll be surprised with the results!

One gray and gloomy winter morning in East Rutherford, New Jersey, the CEO of the company where I worked called me to his office unexpectedly. When I walked in, the vice president of sales, an intense and relentless executive who was my direct boss, was cracking a rude joke. The CEO just nodded as if he'd already heard all the tasteless jokes in the world. They both greeted me warmly, like a long-lost son.

I sat down next to the VP of sales, who gave me a reassuring smile; not a good sign.

The CEO turned to me with a serious look. "We need to expand, and you can help us."

He looked at me eagerly, as if expecting me to produce a grand business plan that no one had ever thought of. I looked

The Builder

at him and nodded thoughtfully, as if in agreement with his favorable assessment of my abilities.

Undeterred, he continued, "We would like you to create a new inside sales team."

Inside sales team? I repeated the phrase in my head; I had never heard it. What was an inside sales team? Were we going to keep salespeople in the office under lock and key? But this was not the time to ask. They clearly expected me to start and lead this new department. I decided to play the game and see where it would take me.

The VP, as if sensing my hesitation, turned to me and said, "You are the right person for the job," patting my shoulder.

I straightened in my seat and said confidently, "I appreciate your trust in me and will be honored to create an inside sales team for our organization. What are the resources needed to make it the finest inside sales team in the industry?"

They exchanged quick glances, visibly satisfied with my response.

"Well, you need to find the right people first," said the VP.

"How many people are we talking about here?" I replied.

"You should be good to go with five new employees."

I continued to push my luck. "What are the revenue targets for this group?"

"A million dollars in sales for every quarter," came the reply.

I made a big show of nodding and sagely considering the numbers. I decided to amp it up a bit.

"I would need ten new people to accomplish this."

They looked at each other and smiled broadly. The mood in the room was getting more cheerful by the minute. The CEO turned to me and said, "Why don't you start with five new employees, and we can evaluate your progress in ninety days?"

I shook hands with them both. The deal was sealed. As soon as I left the room, I investigated what I had just signed up for. In due course, I was running the all-new inside sales team, generating the revenue targets we had agreed on.

My intuition told me to jump right in when it was clear that these top executives trusted my ability. That was good enough for me, and I went along for the ride. Trust yourself to do a fantastic job, even if you don't know how when you start. Fake it 'til you make it.

I could have rested on my laurels after transforming the annual conference and setting up the inside sales team, but something kept bothering me. Our company lacked brand recognition and there was an almost nonexistent awareness of what we did. I thought long and hard about how to change that and concluded that we needed to be featured by a major news network. This, I knew, would dramatically increase awareness.

After a long and exhausting effort to convince a major network to do a story about the company, I convinced a reporter at CNBC to come and film a short segment. I kept the whole thing under the radar, not sharing it with my team or my boss, thinking it would be better to go through with it without asking for permission I might never get.

On a freezing Sunday morning in winter, I drove to the office. There were no cars in the parking lot when I went into the dark building, opened doors, switched on lights, and turned on the coffee machine. Thirty minutes later, I got a call from my contact that the television crew was downstairs.

The Builder

The crew consisted of a reporter, a sound technician, and a camera operator. We started with video shots of me at the entrance next to the company's logo, then went to the boardroom where my laptop was linked to the projector. I was nervous; this was the third time I'd bet big on something that could either make me a hero or get me fired.

After the first few minutes of the interview, I relaxed. The reporter was more interested in juicy stories about what our software could do than technical explanations of how it worked. I was happy to oblige. By the time the interview was over, I had even started to enjoy it. The crew packed up in record time and I was told the segment would air the next week. Several days later, I got a call from my contact at CNBC letting me that the segment would be on the next day.

I had to call the CEO—the guy who promoted me. He was surprised that I was calling so late in the evening. I got straight to business and told him that his company was going to be featured on national TV the next day.

"National TV?" he said, incredulous.

I informed him that we would be featured in a five-minute segment on CNBC. There was a long, uncomfortable silence on the other side.

"This should have been preapproved by me. I will need to inform the board of directors." He disconnected the call without saying goodbye.

My heart sank and I began to worry. What if the segment was negative? What if they made fun of the technology? We were a publicly traded company, and negative exposure could spell dire news for the share price.

The next day passed like someone old and frail trying to climb a steep hill. CNBC called and let me know that the segment would air sometime between seven and eight P.M. I sent an email to the CEO. No reply. At seven I opened a bottle of wine, hoping for the best. I noted that this was middle of the night in Israel, where the CEO lived, and imagined that he couldn't be too happy to be awake.

As luck would have it, it was the last segment that aired, at five minutes to eight. It started with me standing proudly in front of the company's logo as if I owned the firm, then moved on to the interview. To my relief, it was a positive piece. The reporter closed by saying our software was "one of best new innovations of the year, and a transformative technology for large corporations."

Just as I finished my third glass of wine, the CEO called. "The board was watching, too. Let's see what happens when trading starts in the morning."

Our share price went up by 3%. More importantly, we landed interviews on CNN as well as in the *Wall Street Journal* and *New York Times*. My gamble had paid off.

Would I do it again? Probably. It's in my nature to be impatient with the way things are. From time to time I need to stir the pot to feel alive. However, I have to keep in mind that this unauthorized CNBC interview could have gotten me fired. Most companies have strict rules about media interviews and who represents the business. It's always a risk when you push the boundaries.

When you make a significant move in your Explorer years, you don't feel the full weight of your decision. There is less on the line—fewer responsibilities, fewer people who depend on you. Taking a major risk in the Builder years, however, is not for the faint of heart. And you can't just jump from one risk to another. Rather, you must carefully weigh the pros and cons. Is the reward big enough to justify the risk? Are you prepared to take on this opportunity? Would it make more sense to start smaller?

Only you can answer these questions, which brings us to the importance of consistent performance. You see, taking a few big risks in your career works when you've laid a foundation of consistent performance and focused effort. It's like building up a bank account with frequent deposits. You're building credit and goodwill. Then when you take a major risk, it's not coming out of nowhere. You have an established record to point to.

Ray and the Worm

There is a delicate balance at play in the Builder phase. You absolutely must take the right kind of professional risks, but at the same time, you need to apply consistency and repetition every single day if you're going to realize your full potential.

Ray Allen is one of the best three-point shooters in the history of the NBA. For the eighteen seasons he played professional basketball, Allen was the first one on the courts at practice and before games, shooting hundreds of times, following the same routine. He didn't practice dribbling or passing or dunking; he had a single-minded focus on shooting three-pointers. When asked why he never changed his routine, he answered, "I am working toward long-term success. I don't get too excited about shots I make because I'm *supposed* to make them. I'm more perplexed when I *don't* make it. Shooting is not a second nature anymore; it's first nature."

Miami Heat coach Eric Spoelstra added this observation: "Our nickname for him is 'Everyday Ray.' He is doing the same thing every day. It's not every other day. It's not some days. It's every single day."

Work on improving yourself in your chosen area every single day over a long stretch of time, and I guarantee that amazing results will follow. It sounds simple, but how many people can commit to improvement every single day? The work ethic and desire for mastery this requires are not common traits. However, if you summon the will and discipline to do it every day, you'll reap the benefits, simply because you'll be one of the few who can.

Dennis Rodman, aka the "Worm," is widely acknowledged as one of the best rebounders in the history of the NBA. Rodman dedicated himself to the study of rebounds at the expense of everything else. Isiah Thomas, Rodman's teammate on the Detroit Pistons, relayed this anecdote: "We were standing in the lay-up line, warming up and shooting, and Rodman was standing back and watching everybody shoot. I said, 'Hey, come on, you have to participate; everybody's shooting lay-ups; you have to shoot lay-ups, too.'

"And he said, 'I'm just watching the rotations on the basketball.'

"I said, 'Excuse me?'

"He said, 'When you shoot, your ball spins three times in the air. Joe's ball spins four times.'"

Isiah added, "That's how far Rodman had taken rebounding: to a totally different level, like off the charts. He knew the rotation of every person who shot on our team—if it spins sideways, where it would bounce, how often it would bounce left or right. He had rebounding down to a science, and I never heard anyone think or talk about rebounding the way he could break it down."

This level of single-minded dedication and focus is what you need to become the best version of yourself as a Builder. The best way to do that is focus on small achievements. If you break your big goals into small chunks and impose artificial deadlines on yourself, you will eventually get to the end of rainbow.

Think about something that represents a step toward building your empire, then commit to it. Better yet, spend money on it, invest in it so you have another incentive to get it done.

Unforeseen things will happen. Distractions will come at the most unexpected and inconvenient times, but you must hold dear to your commitments. If it means that in the last week before your deadline you need to pull a few all-nighters to come through, so be it. Do whatever it takes.

Once you get into the habit of setting and meeting internal deadlines, you'll be able to establish a valuable routine that will serve you well in life. And if you find out that the deadlines you set for yourself are too aggressive, relax them so you don't run yourself ragged.

Better than your Immediate Competition

Society conditions us to idolize disruptors, people who come up with surprisingly innovative ways to change the world. But how many people do you personally know who can come up with a new iPhone or a new e-commerce platform? People like Steve Jobs and Jeff Bezos are as rare as Leonardo da Vinci. It can be inspiring to read about them, but their success stories are so far-fetched that they can have the opposite effect. Rather than inspire, they can discourage us from doing something extraordinary on our own terms. You need to figure out what success means to you, not how you'll become the next Steve Jobs.

Your plan doesn't have to be complicated. Let's say you're opening a coffee shop in your hometown. You don't have to serve the best coffee in the world; you only have to provide better coffee and a better experience than your direct competitors. If you have one competitor, this should be easy. If you live in a large city, it will be tougher. Still, you only have to be better than the coffee shops around you, not all the coffee shops in the entire city.

Now if your dream is to source, roast, and prepare the best coffee in the world, then go for it—but pursuing perfection is rarely effective. Simply having higher standards than those around you will suffice. This might seem like strange advice in a culture obsessed with perfection but remember: perfection is a myth. It's just another distraction, and it's a poor excuse for not doing the things that will get you closer to your goals.

You must do things repeatedly over a long stretch of time to get profoundly good at them. There is no way around this. One of my cousins is a successful partner at a major law firm. Years ago, when I asked him if there was one thing that made him successful, he said without hesitation, "Once you find out what you are really good at, just keep doing it without looking left or right."

The Builder

This is the best advice for the Builder phase. Don't let anything stand in your way. Keep on doing what you need to be doing, and slowly but surely you will see the fruits of your labor. This phase calls for a focused, consistent attack over 18 years, with very few detours along the way. This life stage rewards resilience, determination, and persistence.

I realize that when you are 36 years old, it's difficult to imagine your mid-fifties. Don't think about it too much; it's too far in the distance. All you must do as a Builder is dedicate yourself to the goals you set for yourself, work toward them without giving up, and take comfort in the idea that when you're 54, you'll be able to switch gears and move on to the Mentor phase. These years of demanding work are necessary for growth; there is no way around them. If you realize this is only one of five life phases and that you'll keep on changing and developing, it becomes easier to carry the daily load.

I am not sugarcoating the Builder phase. It will test your resolve repeatedly. Still, there are many joys in raising a family, overcoming challenges, moving toward your goals, and celebrating your victories. This phase is not meant to be exclusively about work. The social and personal relationships you have nourished will sustain you and allow you to replenish your energies as you move forward. Put in the time and effort to achieve your goals inside this long window of 18 years so you can transition to the Mentor phase in your mid-fifties.

Playing Chicken

The Builder stage was the most stressful time of my life. I had to juggle my responsibilities as a father and husband with the demands of starting and running a business. I realize now that it was an enormous effort. It would have been easier if I'd felt like I could focus only on work during these years, but of course I wanted to spend as much time as possible with my family as well.

This dynamic created conflict. Luckily, my wife took on the lion's share of raising the children so I could focus on building the business. For Odelia, it was all about building a solid foundation for our three kids, even if it meant that she practically gave up on her career as a fashion designer. We all must make tough decisions in life. Anyone who tells you otherwise is lying, pure and simple. Odelia decided the best investment she could make was in raising our children the right way, and she poured every ounce of energy and creativity into this massive undertaking.

I quit my job as the head of marketing for a publicly traded tech company at the age of 36, which I see now as the beginning of the Builder stage. It wasn't an easy decision, what with everything that was on the table: a generous salary, bonuses, stock options, status. The timing of my departure also happened to be months before the worst financial crisis in modern history. I decided to use my savings and not take out any loans to finance the creation of my new business venture.

The one thing I did not fully consider was how long it would take to bring in new clients. I remember sending myself messages from my cell phone to my email application on my laptop to check whether I was properly receiving emails, because my inbox was empty—despite hundreds of emails I'd sent out, desperate for new business.

For whatever reason, I never considered quitting my fledgling company and looking for another corporate job. Was it pride that prevented me from doing that? Perhaps, but I don't think so. More than anything, it was a prevailing sense that this was one of my success trains, and I needed to see where it would take me—even if it ran me into the ground.

It was gut-wrenching to see our savings depleted month after month with nothing coming in. After a while, I moved everything we had to the checking account and stopped looking at it; that was the only way I could manage this difficult period. Our family savings were almost bled dry, and I had only enough cash to burn for three more months before the dream of running my own business would go up in flames.

Nothing seemed to be working; no one was returning my phone calls or emails. Then Lady Luck intervened. Don't let anyone successful tell you that luck is not a primary force in their life. You can't summon or control it, but without it, you're dead in the water. Unexpectedly, someone returned one of my desperate phone calls. It was a small software company outside Philadelphia. The money I received from this firm was a lifesaver, and I will never forget it. The two founders saw potential in my services and signed me up as their outsourced head of marketing.

This was the first client that got me into the consulting business. It allowed me to pay the bills and slowly build my business while helping them realize their market potential. Two years later, with my modest help, the founders sold their company and retired. Their bet on my abilities paid off for them and gave me the initial push that created Ignite Advisory Group.

Developing an attitude of "I will continue with my journey, come hell or high water" will help you tremendously as a

Builder. This phase, more than any other period of your life, is about believing in yourself. This mantra should permeate every fiber of your body, even if your hard work seems to be leading nowhere.

If you are considering starting your own business, keep in mind that it's a nerve-racking affair. The early years are brutal. Your friends and colleagues may tell you to "grow up" and "look for a real job," whatever that means. Brace yourself for many moments of lingering self-doubt about what you are trying to do. This is normal. But at the exact time when you need people to believe in you, you will start to hear that you should stop this nonsense, quit whatever you are trying to do, and just get on with a "normal life."

These moments will mount up when the pressure is highest on you, but the right attitude can save you here. Tell yourself, "The hell with it! I have paid a real price to do what I am doing right now, and there is no way that I am giving up so early in the journey."

Some might say that this is not a responsible approach. I submit to you that this is often the *only* way to move forward: by taking on big risks, going for a roller-coaster ride, and seeing where this train will take you. You must double down on your decisions in the Builder phase; you must commit if you want to build something of enduring value.

Throughout this difficult period, I was adamant that my company would do one thing: create and run game-changing customer advisory boards for leading corporations. That's it. I told my team that we would not get involved in branding, or search engine optimization, or public relations, or anything else. The general response from my friends was deep skepticism.

"How can you make it with such a narrow focus?"

"A consulting company needs to do many things to be successful."

"A niche like that will never work. There is not enough demand for it."

Yet I was convinced that if we could learn, through repetition, how to create the best customer advisory board programs in the world, there would be strong demand for our services. It was a lengthy process of trial and error, but by doubling down on one niche, we established Ignite as the leading global consulting firm in this area. Every time we learned something new that worked, we immediately adopted it and added it to our process. Every time something didn't work, we took it out. Do that enough times and you'll have a battle-tested, proven process for getting things done effectively and efficiently.

What you do has value, even if no one seems to notice or appreciate it right now. It is difficult to believe this in the face of contradicting evidence, but remember that your years of dreaming and exploring have led you along your unique path, and by applying yourself, day in and day out, you will get where you need to go.

Consider my father's belief that every single person has three success trains that are coming to take you, and only you, to where you need to go, to what you need to become. How do you prepare yourself to spot your trains as they pass by? And if you *do* spot the right train for you, how do you make sure that you'll jump on the one that calls your name, that has the potential to transform you?

As time passes, we all recognize the missed opportunities that could have changed the trajectory of our lives; shadows of the past that keep teasing us with "what ifs." It's easy enough to miss the first train. Make sure you catch the second or third train that will come for you.

The Longest Commute

One tradition I have instituted in our family is taking a trip with each child when they are about to graduate from high school. It has nothing to do with summer vacations; it's just a chance for uninterrupted time with each kid, away from school for them and away from work for me.

My daughter wanted to go to Japan, so there we were, sitting in a bullet train late in the evening, going from Tokyo to Kyoto. Unexpectedly, a young Japanese man started talking to us. He was dressed in a navy-blue suit and his black hair was lustrous and full. This was an unexpected turn of events, since most of the Japanese people we met were exceedingly polite but avoided direct conversations.

"Where are you from?" he asked us in clear English, smiling broadly.

"From the United States," my daughter answered.

He nodded knowingly. It turned out that this young man, a paralegal in a big law firm in Tokyo, had the longest commute I'd ever heard of: four hours each way, every single day, without missing a beat. He woke up at four A.M., caught the four thirty train, and arrived in Tokyo at eight thirty. He put in a full workday until six P.M., socialized with his peers and managers until eight, then caught a train. He arrived back home

The Builder

at midnight, got four hours of sleep, and moved on to another grueling day.

When I asked about his plan for the next couple of years, he smiled widely, as if he were in possession of a secret known only to a few.

"I am going to continue like this until I get a promotion."

"And when will that be?" I asked.

"In five years," he said proudly, as if he'd already received the promotion.

My daughter asked, "When you have more money, will you move to Tokyo?"

He laughed like that was the funniest joke he'd ever heard. "Tokyo?" he repeated between bursts of laughter, covering his mouth. "*Tokyo?!*" When he stopped laughing, he told us his master plan. After getting the promotion, he planned to move his family to a town three hours from Tokyo, decreasing his commute to six hours each day. The next promotion, which would take place ten years in the future, would enable him to move again, this time to a suburb only two hours away from work. He made it sound as if getting down to a four-hour daily commute would be a walk in the park.

At least he had a solid plan. It could very well work for him. I said, "Just curious. What do you do during the eight-hour commute every day?"

"Well, I sleep for an hour each way," he said. "The rest of the time I split between work-related stuff and personal development."

"What do you mean by personal development?"

"Learning English and Spanish. This will help me move to the international taxation unit at our firm."

I was impressed. This young man has committed to a grueling schedule over a ridiculously long stretch of time. He was also actively improving himself, day in and day out. I had no doubt that he would be able to achieve his goals. Anyone with that kind of discipline will get far in their journey. But most of us would not be able to maintain such a grueling pace for couple of months, let alone years.

The truth is that as a Builder, you don't need such a heavy workload. The plan is not to work eighty hours a week for 18 years, but to sustain your effort without overworking yourself. It's not just sheer effort that counts here. Having fun, socializing, spending time with loved ones, and taking time for yourself are all important for your well-being. Just don't forget the overarching theme of this stage: Buckle down and get it done.

Adopt a mindset that lets you get things done, then develop simple techniques such as minimizing distractions, saying no so you can focus on your priorities, and spending less time in front of screens and more time on what is profoundly important to you.

Ask yourself regularly how you're doing. Where do you need to be at the end of your Builder phase? What is the next mile marker? Are you getting closer? If not, what can you do to make it happen? What should change? These are the kind of questions that help you continuously assess your progress on a monthly and yearly basis.

What doesn't get measured doesn't get done. If you don't set goals for yourself and measure your progress toward them, you'll be spinning your wheels. Write down your Builder goals, then make copies and leave them in your pockets, your purse, and in places you'll regularly see them. Whenever you're looking for your keys or spare change or a receipt, you'll come across a reminder of what's important to you—of what you are trying to achieve beyond your day-to-day existence.

By the end of your Builder phase, you should have an overarching goal for yourself, along with monthly and yearly goals. I wouldn't get as granular as weekly or daily goals; that resolution is too specific. You need a broader view of your life.

The Walk of Shame

The secret sauce to the Builder phase is staying true to yourself and not compromising your values in challenging situations. Life will test you repeatedly; it's easy to toe the line and be like everyone else. Staying centered and keeping your cool will go a long way toward building the confidence you need to succeed.

I spent the last few years of my Explorer phase working in hotels, then decided to jump ship and work for a tech company. This was an unusual move for me, as my math scores in high school might suggest, and I didn't know much about the technology industry. The firm's cramped headquarters had small offices along narrow corridors; my office was at the end of one. If two people passed each other, one had to turn sideways to let the other person by.

I quickly learned the unspoken rule: stay as late as possible. My colleagues were routinely there until ten P.M. Late in the evening, many employees gathered in the kitchen preparing meals, talking about dream vacations, retelling bad jokes. A few surfed the internet, and some fell asleep in front of their computers, waiting for time to pass.

I stayed late every night during the first couple of months, even though it was completely foreign to my nature, but I became quickly disillusioned. I wanted to spend time with my wife and our new baby, and the countless hours in the office dulled my senses, making me feel like a robot on a dazed, unclear mission.

One day, when the clock struck six P.M., I shut down my laptop, took my bag, closed my office door, and was about to leave—but the bespectacled person in the small office across the narrow corridor looked like he'd just seen a ghost. His gaping mouth and shaken expression robbed me of my confidence. I went back to my office, turned the laptop back on, and dutifully stayed until ten P.M. like everyone else.

Another week passed. I gathered my courage for another escape. This time, I didn't give in to the death stare of my colleague—I headed down the long corridor toward the elevators. But it had turned into the walk of shame. Every time I passed an office, someone called out to me.

"Enjoy your vacation!"

"What, working half a day today?"

"Did you win the lottery?"

I pressed forward to the end of the hall. My manager's office was right next to the elevators, and unless he had an important meeting, his door was always open. When I passed his office, I heard my name.

"Eyal, can you come in? I wanted to talk to you about something."

I walked in and he motioned me to sit down.

"How's your day?" he asked.

"Fine," I nodded.

"Can you give me an update on all the projects that you are working on now?"

What is he talking about? It would take an hour to get through everything.

He didn't move or flinch. I sat down, took my laptop from my bag, opened it, and started reviewing my projects. After ten minutes he abruptly stopped me, telling me that he had a meeting he had to attend. I nodded and left the building with an uneasy heart.

This routine continued for a couple of weeks before everyone on my floor seemed to come to the realization that this was how I was going to play the game. After less than a year, the company relocated me and my family to New Jersey, where I started the next chapter in my journey.

The lesson was straightforward: Even when it's extraordinarily hard to stay true to yourself, don't give in to pressure. Don't conform if you don't believe it's the right thing to do. Let your individuality and personality shine through. Remember that while you're staying true to your values and principles, you need to do your job at the highest level possible. The world has extraordinarily little patience for someone with an attitude and sloppy standards. Be the person who performs at a high level while not giving in to unreasonable external pressures and demands.

A Winning Approach

If you dedicate 18 years of your life to building your future, getting things done, and creating something valuable, you'll move on to your Mentor phase with confidence. You have these 18 years to fulfill your destiny, prove to yourself that you can do it, and build a foundation for the rest of your life. When you hit 36, act like you're on fire, with an unrelenting drive to accomplish your goals. You won't let anyone or anything stand in your way.

This mindset will make you dedicate yourself fully. You don't have to run at full speed for forty years—just run as fast as you can for 18. If you apply yourself from 36 to 54 as a Builder, by the time you hit 54, you can look back at all you've accomplished with an immense sense of gratitude and satisfaction. And the best part? You won't have run yourself into the ground. You'll still have the energy and stamina to keep on moving. You will not exhaust yourself by running the rat race until your late sixties or early seventies.

Whenever you build something of enduring value, you must expand a great deal of energy over an extended time. You are building a solid foundation for yourself and your loved ones. This is the right time and place to apply intensity and focus to your life.

It's a tall order, but it can be done. Doubling your efforts now doesn't mean you'll need to work eighty-hour weeks for 18 years. It does mean that you'll need to get serious about your goals, manage your time effectively, and take great care of yourself and your loved ones. A rich social life is important to your well-being, and the relationships you cultivate throughout your life will serve you well as a Mentor and a Giver. But do you really need to go out three times a week? Do you need to accept every invitation? If you say no from time to time, you can work toward your goals while everyone else is socializing.

Working halfheartedly for forty years is not the answer. Developing the will and habits that allow you to focus and

The Builder

be productive is. If you do that during the 18 years of your Builder phase, you will get quality results. Very few people think like this, let alone live like this.

We become what we think constantly about, and if you apply yourself, go the extra mile, and do what's necessary to make it happen, you will be in great shape when you reach your Mentor phase at age 54.

Transition Plan

One of the traps of the Builder phase is that if you succeed in reaching your goals, it's difficult to change gears. Once you're on the fast track, it is incredibly difficult to slow down, look around, and contemplate your next move. Add in the financial rewards and a lifestyle to which you've become accustomed, and it is clear why successful people are reluctant to change what has worked so well for them. Shifting your focus will not be easy; we tend to cling to what we have unless we have good reason to let go. Most of us do not jump at the opportunity to change, especially as we get older.

In my experience coaching people in their forties and fifties, the all-too-common midlife crisis is a call for help, for reclaiming a lost sense of purpose. Most people start working in their early twenties, and when they get to the Mentor stage, they already have been working for thirty years. Even if they've met their professional goals, they have a sense that there's more to life, that they need to be more. This vague feeling of dissatisfaction can quickly become panic when chasing material possessions no longer satisfies. People yearn for an opportunity to reinvent themselves, but they don't realize that the way forward is in sharing—in guiding younger people who are at the beginning of their journeys. In that direction lies salvation, because helping others achieve their dreams is a noble way to honor those who helped you achieve yours. Focusing on other people's dreams will give you a new sense of purpose. To do that, you need an ironclad plan when turning 54. You'll need to determine in advance how to make the critical transition from Builder to Mentor, because the shift away from hard work, rewards, and daily routines is not straightforward.

Keep in mind that moving to the Mentor phase doesn't mean giving up your regular sources of income. I still own and manage Ignite Advisory Group, for example, but I've delegated many of the daily responsibilities to my talented team to create time and space for working on the Principle of 18.

When you are successful at what you do, it's tempting to keep doing what you've been doing. Everything in the universe, from your partner to your friends to your common sense, will scream at you to just keep making hay, to not change a thing, to ride the wave all the way to an undefined shore.

Resist this temptation. Failing to make the switch to the next level means something significant will be missing from your life. Deep in your heart, you'll know the time has come to make a difference in other's people lives by sharing your hard-earned wisdom with those who need it most.

Stepping out of the Builder phase into the Mentor phase is not a natural transition. It's a forced intervention that you will have to introduce into your life. No one else is going to do it for you, and unless you have this transition point in your mind, it will slip from you as fast as a river into the desert.

Take the high road by shifting gears at the right time instead of getting stuck in the same gear forever. A dynamic outlook on life forces you to see when you need to pivot so you don't get stuck in a twilight zone. Move on with your life, write your next chapter, and help other people realize *their* potential. You have been successful in the Dreamer, Explorer, and Builder phases. Changing from a Builder to a Mentor is the next step in your personal development.

Key Ideas for Builders

You have three success trains. Learn to spot them as they approach by keeping an open mind and considering all options. Jump on the trains that call your name. Minimize your regrets by trusting your intuition.

Learn to take calculated risks. You will get nowhere without taking a few big risks. Start small and expand your capacity for risk. Spotting the right opportunities is only half of the equation; you'll have to take risks to succeed.

Double your efforts, but don't go crazy. Regular, everyday effort doesn't count in the Builder stage; that's what everyone else is doing. Dig deeper and aim and to sustain your intensity for the duration of the Builder phase to achieve meaningful results—but don't forget to nurture robust social connections.

Find one person who believes in you. All you need is someone who will take a chance on you, an opening you can wiggle through. From there it's up to you to widen that window into a breakthrough that could change the course of your life.

Play to your strengths. Don't focus on your weaknesses, but instead, hone your strengths through repetition until you become unbeatable. Focus on the one area where you can become the world champion.

Have an exit strategy. Moving from the Builder to the Mentor stage is counterintuitive. Prepare yourself for this mental shift by learning what it takes to become an effective Mentor.

THE MENTOR
Sharing Your Knowledge

——— *54 to 72* ———

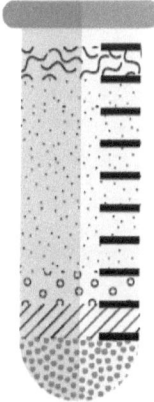

54 to 72
Mentor

*"A mentor is someone that allows you
to see the hope inside yourself."*
—Oprah Winfrey

NORTH STAR

There comes a point in everyone's life when we must look back, assess, and evaluate all we have done so far. Once you reach your mid-fifties, it's time again to shift gears and to start sharing our hard-earned skills and knowledge with the Dreamers, Explorers, and Builders of the world.

The biggest mistake you can make at the beginning of your Mentor stage is to continue to operate in the same way you have for the last 18 years. Carl Jung, the noted Swiss psychologist, summed it up best: "We cannot live the afternoon of our life according to the program of life's morning."

Continuing to do the same things you've done for the last 18 years without considering how to share your experience with younger people is a recipe for a midlife crisis. This dreaded crisis is a cry for meaning, for reclaiming a sense of purpose after years of arduous work. Ask yourself—how long can you continue to produce, day after day, without sharing what you've learned?

Here in the United States, we cherish work to the point that it becomes our central identity, our sole purpose in life. Americans work longer hours, take fewer and shorter vacations, and receive fewer retirement benefits than people in other rich nations. What's wrong with this sad picture? People who lack a master plan just keep doing the things they've always done. They don't consider the alternatives. Society has conditioned us to accept certain "realities" as facts of life.

Keep in the mind that as a Mentor, you can keep doing what you did as a Builder. You can retain your sources of income. The difference is that your focus will shift from building your empire to sharing your experience with the intention of guiding those who need it most.

The Principle of 18 allows us to focus on specific themes and assume different identities at each stage of our lives as we strive to connect the generations in one holistic system. Is it a coincidence that when you are introduced to someone in their thirties, forties, or fifties, one of the first questions they ask is what you do for a living? The Principle of 18 introduces a new paradigm and invites you to start conversations with a different set of questions.

- What do you dream about?
- How do you dream about it?
- What are you exploring?
- How are you exploring it?
- What are you building?
- How are you building it?
- Who are you mentoring?
- How are you mentoring them?

On Becoming a Mentor

In my coaching practice I hear many stories about how people became Mentors without even realizing it. People are usually not aware of following a grand plan, but the stories always start with a compelling dream followed by a lengthy period of exploration. Then a plan emerges as the person seizes an opportunity and starts building their empire with tenacity and determination. Around the age of fifty, they start to expand their focus to helping others while keeping their sources of income.

The role of the Mentor is critical to this system's success. Their guidance is the rocket fuel that propels younger generations to pursue their dreams and realize their ambitions. As a Mentor, you play a significant part in shaping the futures of younger people. I believe it's your obligation to give back to society.

Many people pay lip service to mentoring others, saying that they gave a bit of guidance to a college student they met at a BBQ, but these are not serious efforts. Anyone can share a bit of wisdom. Mentors take an active and long-term interest in the people they coach.

By the time you're 54, you may already be thinking about the legacy you'll leave behind and what you have yet to achieve. It's too early to become a pure Giver, but as a Mentor, you have valuable skills, connections, and life lessons that Dreamers, Explorers, and Builders could benefit from.

If you fail to reinvent yourself as a Mentor after your Builder phase, you'll miss the opportunity to evolve into a better version of yourself. Effective mentoring not only helps others achieve their dreams, it also has positive effects on the Mentor in both the short and the long term. In supporting others, we establish a stronger sense of well-being and an expanded perspective on our own capabilities.

The challenge of moving into the Mentor phase is that of identity. As Dreamers, Explorers, and Builders, our identities are intuitive—a part of who we are. We dream for 18 years, explore our dreams for 18 years, and build our castles for 18 years. But once we get to our mid-fifties, it can be a significant challenge to expand upon the Builder identity and assume the role of the wise Mentor. We become attached to the story we've been investing in for all these years: that timeless tale of realizing our dreams, making things happen. We can be reluctant to let go of that familiar identity and exchange it for something unknown.

There is another path. Changing your identity is a decision you can make *today*. As the next story illustrates, even people society has written off can make the switch to being a Mentor.

Until ex-con Randy Rosa turned 54, he couldn't shake his criminal background; he'd spent the first half of his life drifting in and out of prison, never far from trouble. Randy's story illustrates the vicious cycle that keeps thousands of parolees from integrating back into society. He says, "As you get defined for stuff because of your record, you just get further and further into what you know best, which would be hustling, robbing, or stealing."

At 54, with nothing but the shirt on his back and a string of prison sentences, Rosa made the bold decision to become a Mentor to at-risk youth in the Bronx. He was all too familiar with the temptations the kids were facing, and he knew he could show them the other side of the coin. Becoming a Mentor changed the trajectory of Randy's life and showed him that it's never too late to switch gears. Guiding others who were starting down the path he walked years before has allowed him to change their lives, too.

An effective Mentor doesn't have to be an exemplary individual. People who have struggled mightily can provide dramatic lessons on what not to do to the young people who need them the most. As the saying goes: "If you can't be a shining example, become a terrible warning."

Dan from Turnberry

Dan was a handsome, tanned, and relaxed man who drove a bright red Porsche to the Miami country club where I was an assistant manager, early in my career. His down-to-earth attitude was quite different from the other members of the club, and he won the staff over easily. Of course, it didn't hurt that he cheerfully handed out $20 bills whenever he received great service. He always had time to talk to the staff, and I often found myself polishing off cold beers with him in the comfortable bar that overlooked the golf course, talking about life and what it takes to succeed both personally and professionally.

Most of the members were in their seventies and eighties, but Dan was in his early fifties. When I asked him what he did for a living, Dan flashed one of his relaxed smiles and said, "Why do you think I'm here three nights a week? I am semi-retired, son." Intrigued, I asked directly, "How did you get to retire so young?" Over the next several weeks, I learned his life story.

Ever since he was a kid, Dan had been fascinated with traveling around the world, meeting new people, and experiencing new cultures. His favorite book when he was young was

Around the World in Eighty Days. He was fascinated by the way Jules Verne told his stories with cool inventions and a sense of sheer exploration. Right after college, where he majored in international relations, Dan set out to travel the world. He spent two years exploring India, China, Thailand, and Japan. Most of his friends thought he had lost it, assuming he had become immersed in a strange cult or was following a dubious guru across Southeast Asia. After two glorious years, Dan knew it was time to get back to the US.

He was twenty-four years old, without a job or any concrete plan, and for the next several years he tried different things: working for a major bank as a management trainee (he hated every minute of it); selling a new self-tanning sunscreen lotion in Miami Beach; becoming a real estate agent. But nothing connected with what he'd always wanted to do: travel around the world, connect with people wherever he went, and make a living at it.

When he turned thirty, Dan took off again, this time for Bangkok, where he befriended a wealthy American who was buying local artwork and selling it in Europe and the US. His new friend was impressed with Dan's energy, work ethic, and negotiation skills, and offered him a job as an art buyer.

Over the next five years, Dan worked side by side with his Mentor. His responsibilities increased steadily, and eventually he bought the business from his friend. He continued to expand his reach and when he turned fifty, he brought in two younger art dealers and taught them how to look for local artists in Thailand, India, and Japan. He took the arduous work of finding and sourcing local artists off his own plate, and focused his energies on selling the artwork to his network of dealers in the US and Europe.

Dan now had extra time on his hands, but he wasn't ready to stop working. He started teaching a course on how to thrive in the art world at a local arts college, sharing his experience and insights with students who wanted to explore this hard-to-crack industry. In his words, "the interaction with the younger students, who have the passion but don't have the first clue on how to get started, brings me untold joy."

Don't Retire Early without a Plan

Early retirement is a fantasy shared by everyone who has worked for an extended time—especially if the work is repetitive, stressful, or underpaid. To retire early is a financial decision, first and foremost; it is not necessarily related to age. If you can afford it, you should seriously consider it. But don't do it without a plan that goes beyond playing golf, gardening, traveling, or spending time with your family. There must be a layer in your plan that connects you to the dreams and aspirations of younger people.

Dylan was the first person I met who was able to retire early. We became friends while competing in a ping-pong tournament when I was in community college in Daytona Beach; he was in his early thirties and looked like a surfer. He had just sold his vending machine company for three million dollars when he invited some of us to his house, a sprawling property overlooking the ocean. The only thing Dylan seemed to do was play ping-pong. He was virtually unbeatable. My friends and I spent time together with him at his house, where there were free drinks, an infinity pool, a top-notch ping-pong table, and a big-screen TV on the patio. But what I clearly recall from that time, aside from his unquenchable passion for ping-pong, was that Dylan seemed to have lost any motivation to do something meaningful with his life.

Retiring at an early age is usually a bad idea. You have too many years ahead of you, which become an ocean of free time that stretches into the distant horizon. There's nothing wrong with reaching financial independence in your late thirties or early forties! But even if you reached all your financial goals as an Explorer, early retirement leaves you with too much free time and allows you to slip into habits that will not move you forward: waking up late because you have nothing much to do during the day, wasting your mornings, taking it easy throughout afternoons that lazily turn into evenings . . .

At this age, you're too young to sit back and watch the clouds move across the sky. But even when you're older, early retirement without a plan can become a messy affair. I met Gabe in St. Paul, Minnesota, when he was in his mid-fifties. He was a stocky man with short hair and an intense look, and he'd sold a start-up in the financial technology space a few years earlier for a cool ten million.

After the dust settled and the money was safely parked in the bank, he considered his options and decided to retire. His only child was in college and his wife was an ICU nurse; he asked her to quit her job and he took her on a luxury trip across Europe. For the next six months, they went to Rome, Barcelona, Paris, London, and Monaco, staying in five-star-hotels, eating in fine restaurants every night, drinking expensive wine—but eventually they tired of that lifestyle and went home to St. Paul.

His wife went back to work in the ICU. She didn't need to work another day in her life, but saving lives gave her a powerful sense of purpose.

Gabe had a different story. He called his old friends, but they were all working, trying to save for their kids' college education and for retirement.

He tried playing golf and hated it. He gave money to charity, watched a lot of TV in his new mansion, napped in the afternoons. He was, in his own words, "a rich guy with nothing to do."

After a year of pretty much doing nothing, he decided to get a job. Starting another company was too much for him; he didn't consider himself a serial entrepreneur and the sacrifices involved in getting a new start-up off the ground didn't appeal to him anymore. He applied to several companies and was turned down; no one wanted to hire someone who didn't need a day job to pay the bills. He finally found a company where the CEO took a chance on him, knowing he might not stay long.

Gabe proved him wrong. He said, "Once I had this job, I was the happiest person alive. Finally, I was able to mentor and guide the younger managers and become part of a close-knit team, working together on important things."

My Mentors

My earliest Mentors were my parents. As I shared before, my father suffered a severe head injury in his late twenties and lost his hearing. His life lessons were painful since he believed in tough love and did not sugarcoat anything. From him I learned the importance of developing a sense of urgency that leads you to get things done *right now*, without delay. When he needed to get something done, he made a big show of getting up from the couch, stomping on his cigarette, and getting to work.

Watching him struggle with medical emergencies while retaining such a strong passion for life was inspiring. I remember him coming out of anesthesia after open-heart surgery and asking for a cigarette while still in a wheelchair. When I told him that it wasn't good for his health, he laughed and told me that after everything he'd been though, smoking a cigarette was the least of his worries. He had faced death so many times the fear was gone. What remained was a proud, stubborn will to survive and live life on his own terms.

From my mother I learned perseverance and grit. She cared for her wounded husband and three young children on a meager allowance for disabled veterans and was able to cope with the crises that came with dizzying frequency. Every time my father was hospitalized for another surgery, our lives were thrown into chaos, but she never gave up on us. She fought each day to keep our family together and raise us to the best of her abilities. I cannot thank her enough for everything that she has done for me.

When I was in the army, my direct officer insisted on keeping me on the medical team even though I did everything in my power to make him regret this decision. Our base was near sand dunes in the south of Israel; a beautiful beach was only five minutes away—but worlds away. For someone who grew up surfing the Mediterranean waves in Tel Aviv, this was a cruel irony. Here I was, next to a pristine, rarely visited beach, unable to experience it. This drove me mad until I convinced another soldier to leave the base with me on the weekends. We took an army jeep to the beach and spent a few blissful hours swimming and surfing until the day I drove recklessly through the sand dunes and lost control of the jeep. It flipped over and sent us flying into the dunes. Onlookers called the military police, and we spent some quality time in military prison. My commanding officer somehow understood my rebellious side, though. He gave me encouragement even as he dished out disciplinary actions.

After the army, I was anxious to explore the world outside of Israel, but I needed a student visa. I found a book in the library that listed all the colleges in the United States, and it didn't take long to see that tuition at community colleges was significantly lower than at four-year colleges. Next to the listing for Daytona Beach Community College was an image of a palm tree. That seemed like an auspicious sign. I immediately enrolled for a two-year associate degree in hotel management.

I arrived exhausted in Daytona Beach after taking the wrong bus from Miami and making ten hours of stops in every tiny town on the way. I had arranged to rent a room for $200 a month, which seemed like a good deal until I saw the room. It was a tiny garage that had been converted into a studio apartment. There was a sink, a small bathroom, and a bed. When I asked about a shower, I was advised to use the showers in the college's gym. It's amazing what you'll put up with when you're young and have no resources.

The next shock came when I started school. I had seen a few movies about college life in the United States, but the students at Daytona Beach Community College were a surprise.

The student next to me, a short and muscular man with long, wavy hair, introduced himself with a confident smile.

"Miguel," he said, extending a hand covered in paint splotches. I shook his hand and asked, "How long have you been here, Miguel?"

"Seven years, bro."

This was a two-year program. I nodded and said nothing.

Miguel continued, "I work as a house painter. That's how I pay for this program, taking a couple of courses each year."

"And how old are you?"

"Thirty-three, bro."

The dean of the hospitality management program, Jim O'Shaughnessy, soon took me under his wing and gave me guidance, support, and encouragement. He had a certain elusive grace about him; he seemed like someone who could easily accomplish anything he set his mind to. He arranged my transfer to Florida International University with a full scholarship.

Every one of us needs people to believe in our potential, who will tell us in moments of self-doubt, "Hell yeah, you're going to make it!" Once we reach the Mentor stage, we need to provide the same opportunities to Dreamers, Explorers, and Builders. We honor our Mentors and honor ourselves when we give back to those who most need our help.

Making the Switch

The switch from Builder to Mentor is one of the two most important inflection points in this system. (The other is the transition from Explorer to Builder.)

Most people don't believe we need 18 years to explore what we're incredibly good at and develop the skills, experience,

The Mentor

and mindsets that allow us to succeed as Builders. Most people also chafe at the idea of changing what's been working for a long time in their Builder phase to become a Mentor.

Assuming a new identity is always laden with challenges and self-doubt, and this switch represents a major change in your life's trajectory—but you should make it if you're going to keep growing and developing. And like any significant life change, you must believe in it to make it happen.

One way is to start small. You don't need to become a full-time Mentor on day one, but you can dip a toe in. One excellent resource for people over fifty who are considering becoming Mentors is an organization called Encore. Another is Big Brother, Big Sister. These are only two of the many legitimate, worthy organizations that can help you become a Mentor; there are dozens in every community, whether local, national, or international. If you look around, you will find the right type of organization for you.

One of the most frequent questions I hear is why someone should make this significant change. What would happen if you just continued to toil away as a Builder until retirement?

Well, nothing would "happen." The sky is not going to open and swallow you whole. Life would continue, as it always does. Most people do not consciously shift gears when they get to the age of 54. Some might be natural Mentors and guides for younger people, but most people don't actively reflect on why it's important to make this switch and assume a new identity.

I believe that it's not only our duty to share our experience and wisdom with future generations, but it's also essential to our growth as human beings. We must embrace this new identity if we want to avoid the stagnation, boredom, and burnout that leads to a midlife crisis or a soul-destroying emptiness in our later years.

Our salvation is in our ability to pass our knowledge to the Dreamers, Explorers, and Builders who are trying to climb the same ladder that we've already climbed. We need to start thinking about this transition when we turn 54.

My son Jonathan met any attempt to make him do something he didn't want to do with the default answer, "I have time."

In his freshman year of high school, when it was clear that he should spend more time on homework and studying for tests, a typical conversation followed this pattern:

Me: "When do you plan on taking school seriously?"

Jonathan: "I just started high school. I have time."

Fast-forward to his senior year.

Me: "When are you going to improve your GPA?"

Jonathan: "I have time."

Me: "And what about the SAT? When are you going to start studying?"

Jonathan: "I have time."

Me: "When are you going to apply to college?"

Jonathan: "I have time."

This answer works like a charm until it doesn't. During freshman year, graduation seems as far-fetched as going to the moon. But there comes a day when you can no longer improve your GPA, or turn in college applications, or take the SAT. You have time—until you don't. In Jonathan's case, a mad scramble at the end drove all of us crazy, but somehow, in a faintly miraculous way, he managed to improve his grades and get a good score on the SAT.

The Principle of 18 gives each of us a broad canvas upon which to paint our life story in five separate chapters. And like any good story, it has a beginning, middle, and end. Although 18 years may seem like a long time, time eventually runs out. Aim to fulfill the promise of each chapter before moving on to your next stage.

This system works best if you follow the natural progression from one stage to the next and prepare for the transitions as best you can.

New Identities

There are four milestone ages in your life: 18, 36, 54, and 72. Each one presents an opportunity to move on and assume another role. Although each new role is connected to what you've done before, each milestone has a distinct and separate purpose.

When you are a Builder, you know exactly what you need to do to reach your primary goal for the next 18 years. There is no confusion; this is not the time to visualize or explore your three big dreams. The same goes for each other stage in this system. There comes a time where you need to decide: "Am I going to be stuck in place or am I going to evolve?"

If you decide to drive past each 18-year mile marker, ignoring the exit signs that point you to the next stage of your journey, you are making a statement. You are saying that you have no intention to change, that you are comfortable where you are, and that you don't welcome the new role your life is begging you to take on.

It's difficult to step out of something you've done for a long time, especially if you're at the top of your game. But knowing when to quit is as important as knowing when to hunker down and reach your goals.

Anne Mulcahy, former CEO of Xerox, is a perfect example. When she was fifty-six, Anne made the undeniably courageous decision to voluntarily step down from her position to clear the way for her successor and continue her journey of personal development. It wasn't an easy decision. As she said, "It's hard. It's not something that happens naturally if you like what you do and you're good at it. You have to set time limits for yourself."

What Anne did next was reverse the order of the Principle of 18. She joined Save the Children and poured her energy into it, flying all over the world on the nonprofit organization's behalf. In hindsight, Anne realized it wasn't the right time to do that: "The need to fill your calendar is so strong that you say yes to things you shouldn't." It was a noble cause, but it didn't come at the right time. After working with the nonprofit for seven years, Anne decided to focus on being a Mentor. She is now helping mid-career women with their professional journeys by hosting twenty-five women in her apartment every month, creating an incredibly supportive environment: "we sit around and drink wine and solve each other's problems."

What to focus on in terms of the "mentoring mindset" will be different for each of us. The first step is to look at what you're good at and think about the best way to share your knowledge. Think about what *you* needed when you were a Dreamer, an Explorer, or a Builder in terms of a role model, advice, and guidance—and then try to be that person. If you could go back in time and tell your 18-year-old self the important things to do and look for in life, what would you say?

Consider what you, and *only* you, could share with younger people. What unique life lessons have you learned? What hard-won skills could accelerate someone else's learning curve? What pitfalls and minefields should they avoid? Sometimes the most valuable lessons are in the bad decisions you made—much like what Randy Rosa is doing with youth from the Bronx.

The key is to establish a transition point around the age of 54 where you consciously start doing things differently and pivoting to a new and exciting phase. Continuing to do what you've done for the previous 18 years will not help you find a deep sense of meaning. If you force this transition upon yourself, it will be one of the best decisions of your life. Being a Mentor doesn't mean that you stop making money; it means expanding your focus and doing something different with your time and energy.

Transition Plan

As you approach the Giver phase, which begins at age 72, you'll need to shift your focus once again: from one-on-one mentoring relationships to championing a cause that will make an impact on an entire community.

Start thinking about all the things you wanted to do when you were a Dreamer and could not, for whatever reason. The next phase will provide a perfect opportunity to try new things. You'll be able to stay relevant by committing to a worthy, noble cause.

The key difference between being a Mentor and being a Giver is that as a Mentor, you're still deeply connected to your career and your profession. You have the most to offer in terms of opening doors, making introductions, and following the trajectories of your mentees while you are still able to directly affect their journeys.

When you get to 72, those connections are not as strong, since you are likely to be a few steps removed from the day-to-day of whatever you were doing before. Your new perspective will allow you to focus not on opening doors, but on volunteering your time and voice. As you'll see in the next chapter, if you haven't found an organization that embodies what you want to do, you can always start your own!

Key Ideas for Mentors

You have a gift to share. As a Mentor, think about the incredible perspectives and life lessons you can share with people at other life stages. In this hurried, digital world, the ability to contribute your time and just *listen* is a rare treat for others. Your value comes from sharing your hard-earned experiences and connecting the dots to help younger generations make better decisions.

Your responsibility is to push people beyond their comfort zones. Your highest value as a Mentor to a Dreamer or Explorer is not in how to get things done, but rather how to deal with negative emotions, cope with setbacks, develop perseverance, gain perspective, and be courageous.

Assuming a new identity is challenging. It is counterintuitive to shift from Builder to Mentor. You'll need to force this intervention.

Start small, then expand. Take baby steps as a Mentor, then deepen your commitment. There's no need to start with a grand plan; you can work towards becoming a full-fledged Mentor over the years.

THE GIVER
Taking the High Road
72 to 90 and Beyond

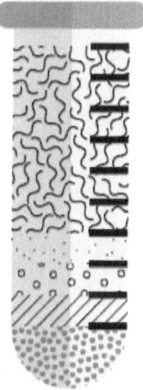

72 to 90
Giver

"We make a living by what we get, we make a life by what we give."
—Winston Churchill

NORTH STAR

Why champion a cause at this stage of your life? What's wrong with playing golf, spending time with your grandchildren, and taking it easy after you've taken care of your responsibilities? You *could*, of course, rest on your laurels, but I believe that's a dangerous place to be for an extended time. It's like surfing in the ocean. When you're waiting for the next set of waves to come in, it's tempting to relax and go with the flow. But that would be a mistake, because the current could carry you away, you won't be able to change course, and you won't get to the next set of waves.

Surfers can never fully relax if they want to be ready for the next wave, and the same is true for Givers. Acquiescing to life's ebbs and flows relinquishes your control over your destiny. Finding your mission as a Giver will allow you to wake up every morning knowing you are doing something that matters.

When you dedicate yourself to giving, you become part of something bigger than yourself, so it's critical to pick something close to your heart. The word "legacy" is loaded; we tend to think about billionaires donating vast sums to universities or hospitals, or people who have made great strides in science, the arts, or business. But even small acts of generosity can have a lasting impact. Many Givers feel like they're not doing enough if they're not operating on the scale of Bill Gates's efforts to eradicate diseases, but thinking in these terms is likely to lead you to inaction. If you don't believe your contributions will have significant impact, why even bother?

When I lived in San Diego, I used to go to a specific spot on a cliff overlooking the Pacific Ocean. I would sit on my favorite bench and stare at the ocean, taking it all in. One day as I stood up to leave, I noticed an inscription on the back of the bench in memory of someone named Sheila—whose birthday was exactly mine, to the day, month, and year. What are the odds? Sheila's gift gives people like me an opportunity to sit down and gaze at the ocean, collecting our thoughts as we take a break from the daily hustle and bustle. I never met Sheila, but her contribution cemented her role as a Giver: someone who worked to improve the lives of others, even though she wouldn't be around to see the results.

Another example of a Giver is Ed, a volunteer at Englewood Hospital in New Jersey. His job is to greet everyone who enters the hospital and direct them to the appropriate department. That's it. But his heartfelt "good morning," along with his big smile, makes a world of difference to the people who come into the hospital anxious and fearful. He brightens their day and reminds them that all is not lost, that there is order in the world—even if it's temporarily disturbed by circumstances beyond their control. Ed isn't investing money in a cause or institution, but he is giving every day.

Beyond the Golf Community

After being a Dreamer, Explorer, Builder, and Mentor, you can finally give yourself permission to fully enjoy the fruits of your labor as a Giver. Maybe you want to spend time with your children or grandchildren, ride a Harley, travel to exotic places, or work on your bucket list. As Laura L. Carstensen of the Stanford Center for Longevity commented, "Older people, knowing they face a limited time in front of them, focus their energies on things that give them pleasure in the moment." There's nothing wrong with that. You've earned every right to enjoy your golden years.

But there's another layer of meaning to explore—a deeper connection to who you can become in the closing chapter of your life.

According to a Pew Research survey, Baby Boomers believe old age begins at the age of 72. But once you're there, what should you focus on? How should you spend your closing chapter? You could certainly take the familiar route of most retirees: develop a hobby or two, travel, and relax into a laid-back lifestyle. Or you could move into a retirement community—somewhere warm with a swimming pool, golf course, and bocce court; preferably without any young people around. For the next twenty or so years, you could lounge by the pool, go on long walks, take yoga classes, travel, and see your family only when you want to.

As with every other life stage, you get what you give, and there's nothing wrong with relaxing into your retirement. I get it! Why work all those years if you can't finally enjoy your free time?

The reality, though, is that it's challenging to find a deep sense of purpose in a life of leisure. And does that strike you as a good ending to the grand play that is your life—quietly passing the time until you fade into the background?

There is another path, one that values you for your insight, perspective, and wisdom: it is the way of the Giver. Even if your focus is on your family, they will look at you differently when you play an active role in giving and volunteering. You can decide how much time to spend on your cherished cause, but whether you do it full-time or part-time, the important thing is to *do it*.

Finding Purpose

A Yale study found that people with positive perceptions of aging lived seven years longer than those with negative perceptions, but it's almost impossible to view aging as positive if you aren't contributing something of value. To remain relevant as a Giver, dedicate yourself to a single cause that you deeply believe in, whether it's an organization, a charity, a school, a religious group—whatever inspires you to give your time and energy. You could even start something from scratch; an animal shelter, for example, if you believe the shelters in your area are not performing the way they should.

Aligning yourself with a sustainable cause will demand your passion and commitment and keep you grounded. Is there a dream you had to abandon when you were younger? As a Giver, you have the precious opportunity to return to it—and to benefit from it more than you could have before. An international study conducted in the United States, Sweden, and Austria found that older adults have more sympathy and compassion than younger people, and that they experience more positive emotional reactions when they donate. Barring serious health issues, many Givers in their seventies possess enthusiasm more befitting Builders. Instead of waiting for others to take care of them, they stride boldly forward. Dedicating themselves to a worthy cause grants them a sense of purpose that is inspiring them to get up in the morning and add value to their communities. They double down on giving back and making the world a better place.

If you aren't used to giving, the transition to this stage can be difficult. As an Explorer and a Builder, you had to dedicate yourself fully to realize your full potential, but when you became a Mentor at 54, you began to give back in a concentrated, sustained way. When you become a Giver, that steady drumbeat becomes a crescendo.

With 18 years of giving as a Mentor and 18 years of giving as a Giver, forty percent of your life is dedicated to giving back. That's the beauty of this system: it allows you to dream, explore, and create for the first half of your life without regrets, knowing that the second half will be devoted to making the world a better place.

Think about where your focus and commitment could add the most value. For example, the AARP Experience Corps, which serves more than 30,000 students in more than twenty cities, has been shown to raise students' critical literacy skills by 60%—and to improve the physical and mental health of its regular volunteers, too.

Safe Water, Free Books, and Personal Loans

Here are the stories of three Givers who have dedicated their lives to worthy causes. They each worked hard as Builders, transitioned to sharing their experiences as Mentors, and finally found a cause to frame their Giver years.

Jin Zidell's mission is to provide safe drinking water to villages in the developing world. While he's at it, he's also having a lot of fun. As he said, "At age seventy-three, I'm having the most interesting and educational time of my life." During his Builder years, Jin worked in his family's steel business. Years passed, and when Jin approached the Giver stage, he had a moment of awakening. Without delay, he decided that his role in life as a Giver was to help underserved villagers with the most basic human need: safe drinking water.

Even though he'd identified his true passion, the enormity of it was overwhelming. In his words, "The next morning when I looked in the bathroom mirror, I was like a deer caught in the headlights. Terrified. I didn't know what the first step should be. I had never started an organization. The idea—along with the fear—gripped me like a hawk with talons in my head. Then I remembered that a hundred years ago, three ordinary women met in a church and declared women should have the right to vote. Well, I'm an ordinary man. With that image, the fear of failure melted away."

To make sure he would bring as much value as possible to his mission, Jin traveled around the world for a year meeting with villagers and the nonprofit organizations that were trying to help them. He recognized an acute need for coordination. The average village in the developing world has only 1,000 residents. With thousands of villages submitting

The Giver

separate proposals for help and funding, the picture of who needed what was murky. Jin and his organization developed a program that could consolidate, prioritize, and follow up on all these proposals. They also created a funding organization to help with projects in the pipeline. When asked the secret to becoming a Giver, Jin says you must "cross the threshold from fear to commitment."

Bonny Meyer has the same level of commitment to giving. During their Explorer years, she and her husband worked in wineries, dreaming that one day they would own their own. It took twenty-five years to fulfill their dream. When Bonny began to prepare for becoming a Giver, she thought long and hard about what brought her joy and which experiences she valued the most, and she decided that her mission was to provide micro-financing to women who can't get traditional loans. Her direct loans make it possible for women to start home-based businesses as well as feed, clothe, and educate their children. This is exactly what Bonny wanted to do: help struggling women who dreamed about owning their own small businesses. Instead of making a one-time donation that would only go so far, Bonny decided to collaborate with women who are motivated to repay their loans and build secure futures for their families.

Bonny's children questioned her approach, fearing that she was taking undue financial risks. According to Bonny, "They were uncomfortable with my social investing at first. Older people are expected to be more risk-averse than young people, but in my family, it's the opposite." Only one borrower in all of Bonny's years of providing loans has defaulted, and Bonny feels blessed by her role as a Giver. The key, according to her, is to "align your giving with your values and life experiences."

Allen Andersson took another path to becoming a Giver. After a long career as a computer programmer, he decided to create rural libraries and internet centers in South America. He had volunteered as a math teacher in Honduras during his Explorer years and later traveled again to South America, where he found rural libraries that were dusty, unkempt, and deserted. The libraries he had in mind were different: "noisy and cheerful, filled with children and adults who explore the open book stacks, do research on the internet, and form community service groups." The activities his new libraries offer connect the older generations with Dreamers and Explorers. His guidance for Givers everywhere is straightforward: "I would urge anyone who wants to do something important in the world to go all the way. Give it every hour you can spare."

A Starting Point

The Giver stage presents significant challenges, the most profound of which is a sense of loneliness. According to the *Wall Street Journal*, every fifth person in the United States over the age of 72 lives alone. Medicare is spending close to $7 billion on what it calls "social isolation costs." But the programs that are available to seniors within their communities focus solely on this age group, and neglect to make the challenging connection to other generations.

When you look into the "senior programs" offered at your local community center, you find that the sole focus is on seniors connecting with other seniors. This is certainly a worthwhile effort to combat social isolation, since strong

The Giver

social connections are associated with a fifty percent lower risk of early death. But what about interactions between the generations?

Everything meaningful is anchored in human connection. As a society, we must find ways to connect Givers to Dreamers, Explorers, Builders, and Mentors, but our culture lacks the framework that would facilitate this. If Givers are going to give back in a meaningful way, we need to open our eyes to the opportunities around us. Connecting the generations *is* possible if we're willing to get creative.

A notable example can be found in Los Angeles, where teenagers from St. Bernard High School collaborated with a group of World War II veterans in an intergenerational writing group. The students wrote letters to their future grandchildren about lessons they imagined they had learned in the war, then read letters the vets wrote to their actual grandchildren. The students and the vets then wrote letters to each other and worked on joint writing assignments together. This project built lifelong friendships between the veterans and the millennials who participated in the workshop.

Another example is found in Givers moving into student housing geared toward retirees on forward-thinking college campuses. Arizona State University, the University of Pennsylvania, Lasell University, and the State University of New York (SUNY) Purchase are among the institutions seeking to bridge the generation gap; SUNY Purchase's campus has a forty-acre assisted-living facility complete with walking trails, a swimming pool, and a performing arts center whose programming brings traditional students and Givers together. In class alongside Dreamers and Explorers, at university events, and in the dining hall, Givers can share their experience and insight with young students who are just starting their journeys. In turn, they can learn what's important to the young people in their communities.

Intergenerational communities are gaining traction outside the academic world, as well. In Two Harbors, Minnesota, multiple programs connect young and old, including an all-ages walking club and a Lego Robotics program that connects seniors and middle school students. The town, which has fewer than 4,000 residents, even introduced free classes for people of all ages to help each other improve technology skills, create radio programs, and build model aircrafts. According to the mayor, "Engaging generations enriches us all."

At the source of human happiness lies human connection; without it, life becomes a dreary affair. The connection between Givers, Dreamers, and Explorers is critical to Givers' well-being and provides tangible benefits to all. These human connections can start with the simplest of things. My fourteen-year-old son, Daniel, has struck up a friendship with a senior citizen who volunteers at a busy intersection near the elementary school in our neighborhood. When Daniel walks our dog Goldie in the morning or afternoon, Judy always gives Goldie a treat and engages Daniel in a short chat. She asks Daniel about his day and what's going on in school and tells him what's going on in the community. What started as an awkward encounter has developed into an easy relationship between Daniel and his "adoptive grandma," as he affectionately calls her.

Connections between Givers and Dreamers can happen naturally if you are looking for these opportunities. In most cases, Givers are best suited to initiate the contact and cultivate the relationship. Reach out and talk to the Dreamers in your community. Organize an outdoor potluck and invite all your neighbors. Engage with the kid who bags your groceries; you never know if they need some guiding words from you. The opportunities to connect are endless, and by focusing on giving, you'll give yourself the greatest gift of all.

Key Ideas for Givers

Remember yourself as a Dreamer. Think about your childhood dreams and aspirations. What could you do to revisit those dreams and involve actual Dreamers?

You can find your purpose by dedicating yourself to a cause. Don't believe anyone who tells you that all you should do is relax and enjoy the final act. You need to be actively focused on finding a sense of purpose at this point in your life.

Seek out connections with Dreamers and Explorers. (Builders are too busy right now.) Get involved with an intergenerational writing program, music class, or anything else that allows you to interact with younger people in a meaningful way.

EPILOGUE
Connecting the Generations

If we think about the stages of our lives as five acts in a play, our goal is to realize the potential of each act. We don't want to have a few good years followed by a precipitous drop. The goal is a steady drumbeat that keeps us filled with joy and gratitude. Such a long and fruitful life requires three things: a solid plan, a commitment to making it a reality, and a belief in living life in an honorable way.

I envision a future where communities around the world organize Principle of 18 clubs. The first step could be inviting members of a particular stage to get together on a weekly basis—for example, Dreamers who meet regularly to share their aspirations, encourage each other, and foster an environment of acceptance and understanding. There's no reason that Explorers, Builders, Mentors, and Givers couldn't do the same.

Some of these clubs would meet in person, others would be virtual, and some would combine the two. They might start with a single stage, such as Explorers or Dreamers, and host events that attract Dreamers and Givers, or Mentors and Explorers. A natural arc would be to start inviting Explorers to Dreamers' meetings, Builders to Mentors' communities, and Givers to all these communities. Givers would be able to hear

Dreamers' hopes for the future and connect with them on what matters most.

The point is, all the stages are connected to each other. No matter where you are on the continuum of life, you can learn from people in other stages. How cool it would be for a Dreamer from Detroit to connect with a Giver from Paris and an Explorer from Lima? Dreamers and Explorers have a ton to learn from the hard-earned experience and wisdom of these incredible Mentors and Givers, who in turn have the time and desire to invest in the future of younger generations.

If this vision of a global community of Dreamers, Explorers, Builders, Mentors, and Givers becomes a reality—and people from all five stages of life begin to interact meaningfully and help each other achieve their goals and fulfill their destinies—I will have fulfilled *my* dream.

The power in the Principle of 18 is in the common language it provides. If you identify just as an "adolescent" instead of a "Dreamer" or as a "retiree" instead of a "Giver," you have no reason to consider connecting with someone at such a different life stage. But if you are an Explorer looking to learn from a Mentor or a Giver, it's an entirely different story.

What if each one of us had a North Star to guide us at every stage of our life, connecting us with our fellow human beings who are on the same journey? We are surrounded by people who can connect the dots for us, who we can simultaneously learn from and help. My hope is that we open our eyes and see all around us the Dreamers, Explorers, Builders, Mentors, and Givers that will help us find our way.

Although the five stages I have outlined in this book might seem black-and-white, they represent a map that can guide

Epilogue

you through your own journey. The truth is that we *already* dream, explore, build, mentor, and give to varying extents throughout our lives. The Principle of 18 simply makes it possible for you to focus on the right thing at the right time, so you can make more sense of your life and find your unique way to add value to the lives of others.

I wish you all the best in your journey of self-discovery, and hope that by taking the high road you will realize your dreams and become the person you want to be!

ABOUT THE AUTHOR

Eyal Danon is the author behind *The Principle of 18*. His other books include *Before the Kids and Mortgage*, a memoir about traveling around the world for a year, and *The Golden Key of Gangotri*, a journey of self-discovery that is set against the backdrop of a perilous expedition into the source of the holy Ganges River.

Eyal is a Columbia University–trained life coach and the founder of the Ignite Advisory Group, a global leader in managing expert communities. He lives in New Jersey with his family, trying to embrace the four seasons of the Northeast after growing up surfing the Mediterranean Sea. He enjoys reading anything by J.R.R. Tolkien, as well as hiking, table tennis, and Japanese whiskey.

Connect with Eyal at www.eyaldanon.com.

www.ingramcontent.com/pod-product-compliance
Lightning Source LLC
Chambersburg PA
CBHW030908080526
44589CB00010B/205